British Association for
BAAS Pamp

American Horror
from 1951 to the Present

Mark Jancovich

Keele University Press

First published 1994

© Keele University Press, 1994

ISBN 1 85331 149 9

Composed, originated and printed by
Keele University Press Services
Staffordshire, England

Contents

Chronology

1951   *The Thing* (dir. Christian Nyby).
       The Day the Earth Stood Still (dir. Robert Wise).
1953   *It Came from Outer Space* (dir. Jack Arnold).
1954   *The Creature from the Black Lagoon* (dir. Jack Arnold).
       Invasion of the Bodysnatchers, Jack Finney (London: Sphere, 1978) This version is slightly rewritten to update the text.
       I Am Legend, Richard Matheson (London: Corgi, 1956).
       Them! (dir. Gordon Douglas).
1956   *Invasion of the Bodysnatchers* (dir. Don Siegel).
       The Shrinking Man (republished as *The Incredible Shrinking Man*), Richard Matheson (London: Sphere, 1956).
1957   *The Incredible Shrinking Man* (dir. Jack Arnold).
1959   *The Haunting of Hill House*, Shirley Jackson (London: Robinson, 1959).
       Psycho, Robert Bloch (New York: Tor, 1959).
1960   *Psycho* (dir. Alfred Hitchcock).
       The House of Usher (dir. Roger Corman).
1961   *The Premature Burial* (dir. Roger Corman).
       The Pit and the Pendulum (dir. Roger Corman).
1963   *The Haunted Palace* (dir. Roger Corman).
       The Birds (dir. Alfred Hitchcock).
1964   *The Masque of the Red Death* (dir Roger Corman).
       The Tomb of Ligeia (dir. Roger Corman).
1967   *Rosemary's Baby*, Ira Levin (London: Pan, 1967).
1968   *Night of the Living Dead* (dir. George Romero).
       Rosemary's Baby (dir. Roman Polanski).
1969   *The Andromeda Strain*, Michael Crichton (New York: Dell, 1969).
1971   *The Omega Man* (dir. Boris Sagal).
1973   *The Exorcist* (dir. William Friedkin).
1974   *The Texas Chainsaw Massacre* (dir. Tobe Hooper).
1975   *Shivers* or *They Came From Within* (dir. David Cronenberg).
       Jaws (dir. Steven Spielberg).
       A Boy and His Dog (dir. L. Q. Jones).
1976   *The Omen* (dir. Richard Donner).
       Interview with the Vampire, Anne Rice (London: Futura, 1977).
1977   *The Shining*, Stephen King (London: New English Library, 1977).
       Rabid (dir. David Cronenberg).
       The Hills Have Eyes (dir. Wes Craven).
       Damnation Alley (dir. Jack Smight).
1978   *The Stand*, Stephen King (London: New English Library, 1978).

Recently republished in an unabridged version.
Halloween (dir. John Carpenter).
Dawn of the Dead (dir. George Romero).
The Eyes of Laura Mars (dir. Irvin Kershner).

1979   *Alien* (dir. Ridley Scott).
The Brood (dir. David Cronenberg).

1980   *The Vampire Tapestry*, Suzy McKee Charnas (New York: Tor, 1980).
Friday the 13th (dir. Sean S. Cunningham).

1981   *An American Werewolf in London* (dir. John Landis).
The Howling (dir. Joe Dante).

1982   *Videodrome* (dir. David Cronenberg).
The Thing (dir. John Carpenter).

1983   *Familiar Spirit*, Lisa Tuttle (New York: Tor, 1983).

1984   *The Terminator* (dir. James Cameron).

1985   *The Vampire Lestat*, Anne Rice (London, Futura, 1985).
Day of the Dead (dir. George Romero).

1986   *Aliens* (dir. James Cameron).
The Fly (dir. David Cronenberg).
Nest of Nightmares, Lisa Tuttle (London: Sphere, 1986).
The Stepfather (dir. Joseph Ruben).

1988   *Queen of the Damned*, Anne Rice (London: Futura, 1988).
Women of Darkness, Kathryn Ptacek (New York: Tor, 1988).

1989   *The Silence of Lambs*, Thomas Harris (London: William Heinemann, 1989).
Sunglasses After Dark, Nancy A. Collins (London: Futura, 1989).
The Abyss (dir. James Cameron).

1990   *Skin of the Soul*, Lisa Tuttle, ed. (London: Women's Press, 1990).
Tempter, Nancy A. Collins (London: Futura, 1990).

1991   *Terminator 2: Judgement Day* (dir. James Cameron).

1992   *In the Blood*, Nancy A. Collins (London: New English Library, 1992).

1. The Genre of Horror: General Theoretical Approaches

From the early days of the Gothic novel, there have been moral panics in response to the horror genre. In 1797, Matthew Gregory Lewis's novel, *The Monk*, provoked outrage, and sections of the text had to be removed in response to a threat of legal action. In the 1950s, there were campaigns in Britain and America which sought to ban American horror comics,[1] and in the 1980s, there were campaigns against so-called 'video nasties'.[2] There was no clear definition of the term 'video nasty', but it was generally agreed that it referred to examples of horror and pornography. These two genres are often associated with one another, and they are frequently referred to in medical terms. They are referred to as 'sick' and 'perverted' forms which corrupt and contaminate the minds of their audience and the social body as a whole. These descriptions, and the attitudes on which they are based, are not limited to a small group of moral or cultural guardians. They have acquired the status of 'obviousness' and 'commonsense', and are shared by people with widely different political sympathies.

This situation has produced severe problems. Not only has it often been used to justify legislation which extends far beyond the realms of these genres themselves, but the supposed obviousness of these genres' undesirability has meant that there has been little real investigation of their forms or effects.[3] In the case of horror, criticism either relies on assumptions about its undesirability, or else it tends to ignore claims about the representation of sex and violence altogether.[4]

This latter problem is related to a more general problem in the study of contemporary popular culture. Critics have either tended to define popular culture positively or negatively. On the one hand, it has been defined as a positive force which satisfies existing interests and desires, or even acts to positively enrich people's lives by informing and educating them. On the other hand, it has been seen as a form of domination. Mass culture theory and much contemporary post-structural criticism – despite their differences – share a tendency to see popular culture as an ideological form which reproduces relations of power and subordination.[5]

In the case of horror, most post-structural critics have claimed that the genre is founded upon a patriarchal fear of female sexuality. Within horror, it is argued, female sexuality is defined as monstrous, and the narrative works to repress or contain the threat to patriarchy which it poses. However, while critics such as Stephen Neale and Barbara Creed both arrive at this same conclusion, it is worth noting that they do so on the basis of different, and even contradictory, evidence. According to Neale, the monster is usually male, but he argues that as women are usually the primary object of its actions:

it could well be maintained that it is women's sexuality, that which renders them desirable – but also threatening – to men, which constitutes the real problem that the horror film exists to explore, and which constitutes also and ultimately that which is really monstrous.[6]

According to this argument, the monster acts to punish those women who are sexually active, and the only women who survive are those who agree to accept the authority of the patriarchal male hero.

Other critics (e.g. Barbara Creed) claim that the monster is usually female, and that it is often a maternal figure who threatens to devour males.[7] According to this argument, horror narratives operate in relation to a patriarchal fear of the mother which originates in the Oedipus complex when patriarchal culture requires the male child to separate himself from the mother (and repress his desire for her) in order to identify with the positions of mastery and dominance associated with masculinity.

As a result, despite their differences, both these critics assert that horror is an inherently patriarchal genre which is 'primarily produced and consumed by men'.[8] This kind of analysis of popular culture has been criticized by such figures in cultural studies as Raymond Williams, Stuart Hall, and David Morley. Though this work originated in Britain, its theoretical claims are not restricted to the British context, and have become very influential with the American academy.[9] These critics claim that mass culture theory and post-structural psychoanalysis ignore – or even deny – the active historical struggles which compose popular culture in favour of the abstract analysis of 'epochs', or even transhistorical conceptions of 'culture'. They agree that popular culture is not simply a positive force which satisfies existing interests and desires, but they also stress that it is not simply a form of domination either. Instead they claim that it is neither an expression of dominant or subordinate groups within society, but rather a site of struggle between these groups.

Drawing on the work of the Italian Marxist, Antonio Gramsci,[10] and the Russian linguist, V. N. Volosinov,[11] they argue that different social groups are in a continual process of dialogue and struggle. Each group is concerned to justify their own interests and aspirations in order to win the right to social leadership. (Gramsci's term 'hegemony' means leadership.) But this leadership can only be won by a specific social group if it is able to address the interests and aspirations of other groups and present itself as the group best able to satisfy them. If they ignore the interests and aspirations of other groups, they will soon lose legitimacy.

Culture is therefore seen as a realm within which different groups not only challenge other groups, but also attempt to incorporate them. They seek to answer certain interests and aspirations, but only within terms that do not challenge their own. However, the interests and aspirations of certain social groups necessarily contradict one another. As Marx argued, for example, the interest of the proletariat and the bourgeoisie are inevitably opposed to one another. The bourgeoisie can only exist on the basis of the exploitation of the proletariat. For this reason, social hegemony can never be finally secured and won. No hegemonic formation can ever resolve all social conflicts. It will have to be reorganized continually to address new challenges. It will never be a fixed structure, but must change and develop historically.

These processes of dialogue and struggle are also identified in the linguistic forms of texts – or utterances as Volosinov refers to them. It is argued that while members of a society may share a common linguistic system, their differing social and economic positions mean that they will interpret linguistic signs in different ways: that which defines 'freedom' for one social group may be seen as 'oppression' by another. As Volosinov puts it, 'differently oriented accents intersect in every ideological sign. Sign becomes an arena of class struggle.' It is this struggle which gives signs their 'vitality and dynamism and the capacity for further development.'[12] For this reason, while the meanings of individual texts or utterances are always defined in relation to other utterances, it is also the case that each text or utterance redefines language and ideology, rather than simply reproducing existing structures. Each text or utterance is a historical development.

If the 'multi-accentuality of the sign' means that no utterance is ever simply a reproduction of an existing ideological system, it also means that different social groups will interpret texts in different ways. For Morley and others, one problem with post-structural criticism has been that it has tended to rely on conceptions about 'The Audience', rather than socially specific audiences, and has thereby failed to acknowledge that texts do not necessarily have the same effect on all readers or viewers. Certainly texts do have 'preferred readings', but for a number of reasons actual audiences may produce very different readings from that which the text itself seeks to initiate. In his work on audiences, Morley identifies three aspects which affect audiences' interpretations. He points out that the audience may not share the ideological positions of the text, and may therefore qualify or even reject that position. However, he also stresses that interpretation does not simply involve the acceptance or rejection of the texts' ideological position. It also involves the relevance/irrelevance and competence/incompetence of different types of materials for different audiences. In his discussion of these latter aspects of interpretation, Morley draws on the work of Pierre Bourdieu, and his study of the ways in which cultural competences and dispositions are differentially distributed within societies.[13] The issue of the relevance/irrelevance of certain types of material concerns the reasons different audiences select material and identify those materials as 'their sort of thing' or not. The issue of the competence/incompetence of certain types of materials, on the other hand, concerns the competence or cultural knowledge necessary to make sense of specific types of material.

Just as the understanding of modernist poetry or abstract art requires specific competences on the part of the audience, so does the understanding of popular forms such as Soap Opera, Kung Fu movies, or horror.

This kind of work is particularly important to the study of horror for two main reasons. First, it suggests that the horror genre cannot be simply seen as a patriarchal form, but that it can be used differently by different groups. It is not always – or even usually – female sexuality which is defined as monstrous. Different groups will represent the monstrous in different ways and representations will develop historically. Second, it also suggests that horror texts do not have a specific effect on their audience, but can generate different responses from different audiences. The moral panics which have surrounded horror over the years are based on the assumption that certain representations have certain effects. For example, some have claimed that horror creates anti-social or aggressive behaviour, while others have suggested that it reproduces the negative attitudes to women in patriarchal society.

The following study will not try to identify a fixed structure which underpins the horror genre and defines it. Instead it will examine the ways in which the genre has developed historically since World War II. If it overstresses the radical or progressive aspects of the genre, it does so as a corrective to other work which overemphasizes its reactionary or conservative elements. It also concentrates on popular and non-canonical texts. Too much work on horror, particular in work on literature, discusses the genre in terms of a small group of relatively legitimate texts, such as the fiction of Edgar Allan Poe or the films of Alfred Hitchcock, at the expense of more popular texts.

2. Alienations: Outsiders in the 1950s

The modern American horror genre which emerged in the period after World War II grew out of a long tradition of American horror, but it also represented a development away from elements of that tradition. Unlike the canon of British literature which has marginalized or excluded horror fiction, the American literary tradition has been dominated by writers working in the horror tradition from the outset. Charles Brockden Brown, America's first professional writer, was primarily an author of horror fiction, and the American Renaissance was dominated by writers of horror and horrific fantasy.[14] Edgar Allan Poe is the most obvious example, but such writers as Hawthorne and Melville also wrote fiction which draws upon the horror genre. Nor was horror a marginal interest for them. Most of their major works used elements of the horror genre. All of Hawthorne's major novels and many of his short stories draw upon the horror genre, as does Melville's classic novel, *Moby Dick* (1851). Since the American Renaissance, there has been a long and enduring tradition of horror within canonical American literature which includes examples such as Henry James's *The Turn of the Screw* (1898), and Charlotte Perkins Gilman's, 'The Yellow Wallpaper' (1899). All of this fiction was produced within the context of a far more general and popular interest in horror, and the first half of the 20th century witnessed a profusion of popular literature and film. Magazines such as *Weird Tales* published the horror writing of Lovecraft and others, while film-makers such as James Whale and Tod Browning at Universal and Val Lewton at RKO produced a series of popular horror films, most of which are now regarded as classics of American cinema.

The horror fiction of the post war period was certainly dependent on this previous work, but it began to free itself from a dependence on the Gothic elements of the earlier period, and tended to place its horrors firmly within the context of the modern world. This change is particularly evident in the 1950s science fiction/horror film where the threat comes not from the past or the actions of a lone individual, but is associated with the process of social development and modernization. The threat emerges from within modern American society, or else is an alien threat which comes from those realms (such as outer space) which American society is beginning to explore and colonize. The threat also tends to be presented as a collective force rather than an individual monster, and it presents the possibility of global destruction, not just the destruction of an individual or small group.

These texts have frequently been attacked for being deeply author-itarian. It is argued that the monster is presented as inherently evil, a force which must be repressed and destroyed by the forces of order. It is also claimed that they associate the monster with Russian communism, and so justify American society and its institutions.[15] These texts are identified as Cold War narratives which legitimate American militarism and xenophobia. An alternative interpretation is possible though. These narratives can be shown to be as much concerned with developments within American society as with the threat of a Russian invasion, and to be specifically anti-authoritarian.

The science fiction/horror narratives of the 1950s emerged from a social and cultural context which had been transformed during the war and its immediate aftermath. During the war, there was a consolidation of the corporate or 'Fordist' modes of social organization which had begun to develop with the New Deal era of the 1930s. This use of the term 'Fordism' is not restricted to the types of labour processes often asso-ciated with Henry Ford, but it refers instead to a particular organization of social, political, and economic life. The depression had lead many to argue that capitalist economic relations had to be managed to prevent social, economic and cultural crises.

The Fordist system developed a bureaucratic rationality in which experts drawn from the state, corporations and organized labour collaborated to regulate social life. This system increased state powers as the state rejected *laissez faire* capitalism in favour of greater intervention in the management of the economy. New fiscal and monetary policies were employed, and the state took greater responsibility for social welfare. Corporations, on the other hand, began to apply the techniques of scientific management to a growing range of activities. They not only regulated the labour process, but also personal relations, training, product design, pricing strategies, and the planned obsolescence of equipment and product. They were also more concerned to regulate the process of consumption through the use of a series of techniques such as advertising.[16]

Fordism was therefore a centrally ordered system in which an *élite* of experts used technical-scientific rationality in an attempt to regulate a whole series of social, economic and cultural activities. It has both been praised as a rational and non-ideological system which was not motivated by special interests,[17] and attacked as a destructive form of domination and control which has been variously referred to as 'the Power Elite', 'the Technocratic Society', and 'Mass Society'.[18] It is this latter type of criticism which can be identified in many 1950s science fiction/horror texts. If many aliens were identified as Russians, it was through a more general association with scientific-technical rationality which also meant that they were frequently associated with the highest levels of the American establishment as well.

In *The Thing From Another World* (1951), for example, the alien being is, in a sense, the catalyst for a more general struggle between its American characters. While the leading scientist, Carrington, wants to preserve it for study, the military group recognizes it as a threat. In fact, the thing is identified with the scientist for whom it represents the ideal of scientific-technical rationality. Carrington's admiration for the thing is confirmed when he discovers that the alien reproduces asexually, and produces offspring who lack individual qualities. As Lukacs claims, the application of scientific-technical rationality to the labour process (and by extension to society as a whole) redefines the individual qualities of human beings as 'mere sources of error when contrasted with these abstract special laws functioning according to rational principles.'[19] Scientific-technical rationality is only concerned with the quality of the workers' output, and attempts to convert individual workers into mere interchangable components within a system which is regulated by experts. For Carrington, individuality, sexual desire and emotion are defined as a threat to rational processes. They must be contained or ideally eliminated. As the alien species lacks these features, he claims that it is 'superior in every way' to human beings.

The fact that the alien species is made up of duplicates also means that it is not interactive, but is directed by a single unitary purpose. By contrast the military group are represented as an interactive community. It is not made up of experts, but of low-ranking and practical people who are constantly at odds with the orders of their superiors, and with the military hierarchy itself. Carrington, on the other hand, is identified with the highest levels of the scientific establishment, the government, and even the military. For example, he is even identified as a primary figure in the nuclear bomb tests at Bikini Atol. These divisions and distinctions are also dealt with through the film's verbal styles. While Carrington takes positions of authority from which he delivers speeches to others, the military group use a style of talking which is common to films associated with its producer, Howard Hawks: overlapping dialogue. This is an interactive mode of speech in which ideas and authority do not originate in the expert, but from the group as a whole. Every member of the group has an equal right to speak, and they each add to, and complete, one another's ideas. Authority does not reside in a single individual, but in the group as a whole. Arguably, therefore, the establishment – particularly the scientific establishment but also the military establishment – are presented negatively. They are associated with the thing in a number of ways, specially around the issue of scientific-technical rationality. The military unit or group, on the other hand, the 'men on the ground', are presented positively exactly because they are identified as a community of practical workers rather than rational experts.

These issues are also related to issues of gender. It is often argued that, within contemporary culture, the irrational and the interactive are associated with femininity, while rationality and authority are associated with masculinity. For this reason, it is worth noting that the female, Nikki, is unproblematically accepted into the military group as an equal, and that it is her use of domestic knowledge that lays the foundation for the plan which will eventually destroy the alien. The use of domestic knowledge in conjunction with scientific knowledge of electricity eventually triumphs, and in this and other ways, the film acts to break down the hierarchical distinctions between the masculine and the feminine, and the rational and the irrational, distinctions which are necessary for the authority of technical-scientific rationality. For this reason, while the alien's monstrousness is related to its reproductive system, it is identified with masculinity not femininity. It is associated with the masculine both physically and through its hyper-rational lack of emotion. Thus, it is not female sexuality which is the problem, but a 'male' system of reproduction which has eliminated the need for recourse to the female. It is also the case that while the alien may be associated with the Russians, it is additionally linked with the highest levels of the American establishment, and the threat which that establishment poses to the interactive group, or democratic community.

There is a great deal of argument over the interpretation of the novel and the film of *Invasion of the Bodysnatchers* (1954 and 1956, respectively). They have been seen as both anti-communist, and anti-McCarthyite. Such apparently contradictory readings are possible because their concern with the spread of conformity within American society was shared by both the left and the right during the period. The right claimed that the social relations associated with Fordism threatened American individualism, and were indistinguishable from communism. The left, on the other hand, argued that McCarthyism and Fordism both sought to repress or exclude dissent.

While Jack Finney, the author of the novel, has denied that he intended either interpretation, his book (even more than the film) concerns the impact of the media, technology and new forms of social organization upon American communities. The novel concerns a local doctor, Miles, who discovers that the people of his home town, Santa Mira, are being replaced by alien duplicates. These duplicates are the same as the original humans in every way with the exception that they lack emotion. As in *The Thing*, it is the alien's rationality and lack of emotion which is monstrous, and this is also linked to its asexual method of reproduction. In the course of the narrative, the leading characters learn that it is their desires and emotions which distinguish them as human, and that need to be preserved.

These differences between the human and the alien are not immediately apparent though. In fact, the novel stresses the difficulty of distinguishing between the two. The problem is that the humans themselves have been conditioned into standardized and rationalized forms of behaviour by American society itself. It is emphasized that the pods are only speeding up a process which would happen anyway, a process which is identified with the media, technology, and existing structures of authority. Within the book, people's behaviour is shown to be conditioned by *clichés* from books and films. Technological systems of communication, such as the telephone networks, are associated with the pods. The drive towards efficiency within American society is presented as breaking down the relationships between people and imposing an order which is 'utterly brainless' and 'inhumanly perfect'.[20] The bureaucratic military authorities have become unimaginative and define people such as Miles as things to be controlled and not citizens to whom they are accountable. Miles's claims do not have authority within the social hierarchy, and he is defined as irrational by all the authorities.

Ironically, rational methods are completely incapable of dealing with, or even identifying, the menace. The pods' duplication of people is so perfect that it can only be detected by those who have had a close personal relationship with the victim, and even then, there is nothing tangible which can be identified. There is simply something missing in their interpersonal relations, something that can only be identified at the level of 'feelings' and 'intuition'. It is therefore significant that it is usually those with least authority who identify the menace such as children and women, while the authorities dismiss these fears as a product of mass hysteria. People's feelings are defined as untrustworthy by the authorities who offer rational explanations which are not only shown to be wrong, but dangerously misguided. In fact, the rationality of the authorities associates them with the pods, and it is frequently the figures of authority who are the first to be duplicated.

In this way, the pods are not simply associated with communism, but with the structures of American society itself, and as in *The Thing*, it is not female sexuality which is the problem but the repression of those features usually associated with the feminine. The novel also identifies gender roles as a product of conditioned behaviour. Not only is it Becky who comes up with the plan which enables her and Miles to escape the pods, but it also relies, at least in part, on her realization that the forms of behaviour associated with men and women are not fixed and determined, but socially constructed through cultural images such as films and literature. In fact, rather than presenting humanity and personality as being founded upon a fixed presence, the novel identifies them with absence, desire, and interaction. These features are also related to the novel's narrative which does not work towards closure and completion. Instead it emphasizes the unreliability of Miles's narration, and suggests that it is not only impossible to rationalize and resolve everything, but also undesirable.

However, aliens were not always presented unsympathetically during the 1950s. In many cases, they were seen to be misunderstood by American society which was in turn envisaged as harsh and unsympathetic. In this way the alien was used to criticize definitions of normality prevalent within America in the 1950s. The best known examples of this type of film were those directed by Jack Arnold in the early 1950s. In *It Came From Outer Space* (1953), for example, an alien craft crashlands on earth and the towns people start being replaced by replicas who seem to lack emotion.[21] The aliens are not presented as evil however. It is revealed that no-one has been harmed, and that the aliens have only disguised themselves so that they can repair their damaged craft. They are afraid that, if humans see them as they really are, they will be misunderstood, feared, and persecuted. In fact, the aliens are presented as entirely justified in these fears. These issues are related to a more general criticism of small town America in the film through an association with the leading male character. He is not originally from the town, and is himself the focus of the town people's suspicion and jealously.

The Creature from the Black Lagoon (1954),[22] on the other hand, concerns a group of scientists who go on an expedition into the Amazon in the search for fossils and encounter the Gill-Man, a living example of animal life's prehistoric attempts to make the transition from the water to the land. The Gill-Man reacts violently to the humans' intrusion into his habitat which is linked with issues of colonization. Not only are the scientists exploring areas which humans have never visited before, they also believe that the knowledge which they hope to acquire will help humans to colonize other worlds.

Their intrusion is also associated with issues of masculinity. The lagoon in which the creature lives is womb-like in its shape, and the water in general is identified with the source of life. By contrast, the male scientists enter it with spear guns and cameras in a way that is associated with phallic aggression, masculine control, and goal-oriented behaviour Their relationship with the water is very different to that of the creature and the lone female on the expedition, Kay. These latter two exist in harmony with the water, and derive pleasure from it. In fact, while the creature is drawn to the women, and conflicts with the males over her, its attraction to her is not associated with dominance or aggression, but a fascination and affection which is stimulated when it sees Kay swimming in the lagoon. In this sequence, the two are associated with one another as the creature swims along and mirrors her movements. The creature's attraction to her is therefore different to that of the males. It is based upon a recognition of its similarity to her and is clearly distinguished from the acquisitive Mark who also competes for Kay with her boyfriend, David. Kay also shares a bond with the creature. Despite her tendency to scream each time it appears, she is also fascinated with it, and seeks to protect and defend it from the male 'heroes' throughout the narrative.

Like most 1950s horror films, *The Creature from the Black Lagoon* was made primarily for a teenage audience which largely identified with the tragic, alienated creature who existed outside the middle-class definitions of normality held by their elders. In fact, the film gives the creature a tragic dignity, and portrays its world as a fabulous romantic realm. If the film's ending appears to present the triumph of masculinity, the emphasis does not fall on the establishment of the heterosexual couple, but on the tragic destruction of the creature, a point which is reinforced by Kay's manifest sorrow. In fact, the final image is not of the human couple, but the dead body of the creature disappearing into the depths of the lagoon.

Jack Arnold also directed the film version of Richard Matheson's classic science fiction/horror novel, *The Shrinking Man* (1956) (filmed and republished as *The Incredible Shrinking Man*, 1957). Like much of Matheson's fiction, this novel concerns a man who is displaced from his usual relationship to the world. Through a freak combination of factors, Scott Carey finds himself gradually shrinking, and as he does so, the 'normal' world becomes strange and terrifying. He begins to feel intimidated by his wife, and eventually finds himself trapped in the cellar of his house, battling against an everyday house spider which now appears to him as a giant monster. These reversals enable the novel to investigate aspects of 'normal' middle-class American masculinity, and to illustrate that monstrousness is not a quality which is inherent within a particular being, but something which is ascribed to it by another being.

This position can also be clearly seen in Matheson's classic vampire novel, *I Am Legend* (1954), in which the leading character, Richard

Neville, is the last human left alive after a plague of vampires has taken over the world. Neville trys to hold onto his definitions of normality, and spends his time in a futile attempt to destroy the vampires. At the end of the novel though, it becomes clear that to the vampires' culture, Neville is as much a monster as they were to his own culture, and the novel thereby illustrates that definitions of the monstrous are always socially constructed, while it also investigates the limitations and problems associated with Neville's concepts of normality. These are presented as both profoundly unimaginative and brutally repressive, particularly in relation to issues of gender. Neville not only fears active female sexuality, but continually directs his sadistic experiments against female vampires, while pathetically holding on to an idealized memory of his aptly named wife, Virginia.

If these narratives work to relativize American definitions of 'normality', the works of the late 1950s and the early 1960s go further in their criticism of American society. They present American institutions as destructive in both personal and global terms.

3. The Emergence of Contemporary Horror

I   Family Horrors

The release of *Psycho* in 1960 is seen by many as a significant break in the development of the horror genre. Such critics as Robin Wood argue that *Psycho* starts a critical trend which identifies the monster with the fundamental institutions of American society, rather than with foreign forces.[23] For Wood, the horror has previously taken place outside America, or else was the result of an invasion by external forces. At this stage, American institutions were seen as the solution to the horrors, not the problem. *Psycho* is said to change this situation. According to Wood, the film identifies the American nuclear family as the source of the threat. It is not 'abnormal' or foreign elements which are the problem, but American definitions of 'normality'.

In *Psycho*, the monster appears to be a 'normal' American teenager, Norman Bates, whose personality is split. On the surface, he appears to be a shy young male, but when sexually excited, another personality takes over which murders the object of his desire. Norman sees this other personality as an entirely separate being, which he calls 'mother', and she is the product of a disturbed mental state which derives from his family background. For Wood, *Psycho* is therefore a critique of the institution which he sees as fundamental to American society, the patriarchal family.

There are problems with Wood's position though. First, as Barbara Creed and others have argued, Norman is not the product of a patriarchal family, but a family which lacks a father and which is dominated by the mother.[24] For these critics, the film does not present 'normal' family life as the problem, but the lack of a patriarchal presence which would sever the bond between mother and child, and allow Norman to develop 'normally'. Rather than a critique of the patriarchal family, they see *Psycho* as an endorsement of patriarchal ideology. This argument overstates the case somewhat. All the families within the film are presented as destructive and corrupt, even the patriarchal families. At the beginning of the film, Marion Crane, Norman's first victim within the film, steals money from a business man who is buying a house for his daughter. This business man is also presented as a domineering and destructive influence. He is buying the house in an attempt to maintain his control over his daughter after her forthcoming wedding. His sexual advances to Marion also highlight the hypocrisy of his family values. None the less, the arguments of Creed and others do require, at the very least, a qualification of Wood's position.

It is also important that the nature of the supposed break is not overemphasized. As we have already seen, American institutions have always been precarious within horror. They are frequently identified with the horrors in various ways. If there were not some fault or problems with them in the first place, there would be no convincing threat.

The focus on *Psycho* as a distinctive case also needs to be questioned. *Psycho* was not unique at this time in its depiction of the family. Similar concerns can also be identified in Shirley Jackson's *The Haunting of Hill House* which was published in 1959, the year before *Psycho*'s release in 1960, and also in Roger Corman's adaptations of Edgar Allan Poe, the first of which was also released in 1960.

The Haunting of Hill House concerns a young woman, Eleanor, who has spent her life looking after her sick mother. She not only feels that she has been dominated by her mother and never had a life of her own, but like Norman, this situation has lead to a series of psychological problems. When her mother dies, Eleanor feels liberated, but she also suffers from feelings of guilt. (She believes that she may have been responsible for her mother's death.) More significantly, her sense of identity is insecure. Longing for freedom, she heads off to join a research team who are investigating a possible haunting at Hill House. But when she reaches Hill House and finds that she is the first to arrive, her fantasies of freedom soon give way to feelings of loneliness, isolation, and vulnerability. When Theodora, another member of the team, arrives, Eleanor immediately attaches herself to Theodora, only to finally feel trapped and smothered by this relationship. Eleanor finds it impossible to find a stable sense of identity, and she swings between fears of being engulfed or abandoned by others. This situation intensifies to the point of madness as Eleanor is drawn to the house, and eventually commits suicide so that she will not have to leave it.

Despite the fact that this novel, like *Psycho*, concerns the psycholog-ical damage done to a child by a domineering mother, it has often been praised as an account of the problems women have in establishing a stable sense of identity. Judie Newman, for example, uses Nancy Chodorow's work on the relationship between mothers and daughters.[25] She argues that unlike the male child which separates itself from the mother and identifies with the father, the female child rarely achieves the same sense of separateness from the mother, but continues to identify with her. As a result, the female child does not experience itself as a sep-arate entity to the same degree as the male. This situation leads to a less secure sense of identity which can be seen in a variety of ways within the novel. Not only does Eleanor continually imitate others in her search for an identity – a strategy which is fraught with contradictions and doomed to failure – she also finds that she has internalized the attitudes of her mother and others, and is continually unsure whether the thoughts she has are her own or derived from others. This problem is also related to her relationship with the house. While she is there, a series of events seem to revolve around her. Eleanor believes that the house is addressing her, but it is also possible that these events are a projection of her own uncon-scious desires – there is the suggestion that she may have telekinetic powers. Finally, at the end of the novel, when she commits suicide, Eleanor's last feelings are of panic. She is unsure whether her suicide is her own choice or whether some other force is compelling and controlling her.

A preoccupation with the relationship between madness, identity and the family can also be identified in Roger Corman's adaptations of Edgar Allan Poe's work. The first of these, *The Fall of the House of Usher* (1960), contains many of the elements of later films. Despite these films' use of Poe, it is worth remembering that any reinterpretation must be understood in terms of the specific period within which they are produced. One not only has to recognize that the turn to Poe's fiction in the late 1950s has as much to do with the concerns of the period as it does with those of the original texts, but also that any reinterpretation will alter these originals, if only by concentrating on some features rather than others. In fact, Corman's films depart from Poe's originals significantly. For example, in contrast to the plot of the original Poe story, Corman's film concerns a young man who comes to the house of Usher to collect his fiancee, Madeline Usher, and take her back to Boston with him. This detail not only changes the function of this character within the story, but also introduces issues of generational conflict which are entirely absent from Poe's original tale. In the house of Usher, the young man encounters Roderick Usher who is obsessed with the evil of the Usher family line, and fears that he and Madeline are tainted with that evil. He feels oppressed by the past and the film is filled with images of confinement and claustrophobia. The action barely moves outside the self-contained world of the house which contains not only bedrooms and dining rooms, but chapels and crypts.

The film makes much of the house's enclosed spaces and underground corridors within which Roderick eventually buries Madeline alive. He wants to prevent her from having children and continuing the family line. The preoccupation with premature burial is a continuing theme through the later Poe films, and like these later films, it is linked to a fear of catatonia. Catatonia is a condition in which the person has all the outward appearances of death, but is still alive. Later films, such as *The Premature Burial* (1961), emphasize the fear of being rendered helpless; unable to move or communicate, but still conscious of the surrounding world and able to feel pain.

The film not only stresses these external threats to identity. The most terrifying threat is presented as internal. Roderick's main fear is that he and Madeline will go mad; that forces within their own make-up will erupt and render them helpless. The preoccupation with catatonia has some of these connotations, but his fear of madness is more explicit. He fears that even his own consciousness is unstable, and that it may be erased by more powerful forces within his own psychological make-up over which his conscious self has no control. The same preoccupation recurs in later adaptations of Poe by Corman. In *The Pit and the Pendulum* (1961), the leading character is eventually possessed by the personality of his father, a cruel member of the Spanish inquisition, and in *The Haunted Palace* (1963) (really a version of H. P. Lovecraft's 'Charles Dexter Ward'), the leading character is possessed by the personality of one of his ancestors.

This concern with the family and with the instability of identity links all three films and was to become one of the central problems within contemporary horror. It cannot simply be explained as the innovation of *Psycho*, or its director Alfred Hitchcock. It was part of a more general cultural process. In the early 1950s, in texts such as *The Thing* and *Invasion of the Bodysnatchers*, the consciousness and desire of individuals were presented as that which was threatening to rational control, as that which it must repress or deny. The rational system had to discipline their desires and discourage people from thinking for themselves. But as American society developed during the 1950s, American industry attempted to control consumption according to rational principles through the use of advertising and other techniques. Rather than repressing or denying desires, it attempted to stimulate specific desires.

As this process developed, it became increasingly commonplace for people to claim that consciousness and desire were now integrated within the system of rational control, rather than threats to it. This situation led to a profound sense of instability as people became uncertain which thoughts and desires were their own, and which were the products of the system of control. The boundaries between the inside and the outside, the self and the system of control became blurred and obscure, and their faith in their ability to resist was questioned.

In fact, while theorists of mass society and culture had claimed that the development of rational control would increasingly lead to a population which was complacent and uncritical,[26] it might be more accurately argued that it led to an increasingly paranoid population who felt that they had less and less control over their own lives, and were more and more suspicious of the authorities that sought to control them. Unfortunately, these conditions also gave them less and less confidence in their ability to change this situation.

During the 1960s, this situation was largely responsible for the shift from secure to paranoid horror which has been identified by Andrew Tudor.[27] According to Tudor, prior to the 1960s, secure horror had maintained a series of relatively unproblematic distinctions between self and other; there was some sense of faith in authority and in the possibility of effective action; and hence, a general tendency to resolve narrative conflicts. In the 1960s though, these features started to disappear, and paranoid horror emerged from a blurring of distinctions between the self and other; a loss of faith in authorities and the possibilities of effective action; and hence, gave rise to horror narratives in which conflicts and problems are rarely resolved, but seem to move inexorably towards complete social or personal breakdown or apocalypse.

For Tudor, family horror must be understood in this context; not as a concern with the family in itself, but as part of a more general crisis of confidence in American institutions. In fact, an examination of family horror after 1960 calls into question Wood's assumption that the family is the fundamental institution of American society. Most of these family horror texts clearly present the family as only one element in a more general series of institutions and processes which penetrate and shape one another.

Ira Levin's novel, *Rosemary's Baby* (1967), for example, is as much concerned with the media and other forms of authority as it is with the family. The novel centres on a young woman, Rosemary, who moves into a new apartment with her husband. There she becomes the focus of a Satanic conspiracy which uses her as a vessel for the birth of the Antichrist. Though it is often seen as an example of family horror, this novel clearly presents the family as part of a much broader series of processes. Rosemary's desire for a family, and her image of family life, is constructed through a series of different institutions, from the Catholic church of her past, to the vast array of consumer images which permeate her world. The novel is filled with references to the media and media events, and these are shown to not only define the terms of fashionable conversation, but also the modes of appropriate behaviour. Rosemary arranges her apartment according to the advice of popular magazines, and her sexual and moral behaviour are learned through a variety of sources, such as *Time* magazine and *The Kinsey Report*.

Nor is it the case that the Satanists challenge her behaviour or beliefs. On the contrary, they rely upon them, and they are themselves representatives of the very authorities on which she has been taught to rely. They are traditional elderly couples, and well respected doctors. During the course of the novel, Rosemary does begin to fear them, and becomes concerned about her lack of control over her own body, or her pregnancy. She comes to feel herself to be the object of a conspiracy who is manipulated by others. But her trouble is that while she fears others control over her, she has no confidence in her own capacity for action. She has no knowledge or resources of her own with which she can resist, and she is forced to turn from one authority to another in the hope of finding some sense of security.

Not only is this attempt ultimately doomed to failure, but it is exactly what the Satanists themselves are relying on. Lacking knowledge of the forces which control her, Rosemary has misinterpreted the Satanists' designs upon her. She believes that they intend to sacrifice her baby, and she struggles to protect it. But the Satanists have specifically chosen Rosemary because of her attachment to the values of motherhood, and they know that this attachment will lead her to protect the baby. The baby which she carries is not intended for sacrifice, but is the Antichrist itself. In seeking to resist the Satanists, Rosemary is doing exactly what they have planned for her. As a result, the end of the novel does not involve the victory of good over evil – these terms have lost any clear sense of distinction. The attitudes towards motherhood which Rosemary has learned from the media and the church lead her to accept the Antichrist as her child, and she agrees to mother it, so confirming the movement towards the apocalypse.

Stephen King's novel, *The Shining* (1977), also places family horror within a broad social context. The novel concerns a man, Jack Torrance, who has a history of alcoholism and uncontrollable rages. These problems are partly the result of a disturbing family background in which his father had violently abused Jack's mother. His weaknesses make it difficult for him to hold down a job, and he finds himself struggling to support his own family which is made up of his wife, Wendy, and his son, Danny. As a result, he eagerly accepts a job as the winter caretaker in the secluded Overlook Hotel, hoping that this job will not only enable him to support his family economically, and allow him to concentrate on his writing – Jack wants to be a major writer – but also allow him to escape the social pressures which are destroying his family and himself.

Ironically, the family's attempt to retreat from the social world only intensifies the pressures upon and within it. Jack begins to undergo a breakdown, believing that the Hotel is encouraging him to kill Wendy and Danny, and he is finally overtaken by a murderous rage. In the process, the novel highlights that the retreat from the social world into a self-contained, protective domestic sphere is not only impossible, but also destructive. In fact, the idea of the family as a haven from the pressures of the social world is the very root of the ideology of the family. It is an unsustainable myth which disguises the social and economic pressures which shape the family.

Jack's breakdown is in part due to his acceptance of his social role as a father. He is presented as genuinely in love with his wife and child, but he is driven mad by his frustration at being unable to perform his economic function as the breadwinner adequately. As he does so, he begins to resent and hate them, and feels that they are a drain and a burden on him. In this way, his social role as a father also comes into conflict with other ideologies of masculinity which he has internalized, particularly the ideal of the heroic, independent male. This conflict is also related to his ambitions as a writer. On the one hand, he craves critical success and popularity, while on the other, he fears that if he achieves them, it will mean that he is not enough of an independent artist. He tends to accept the ideology of the artist as a struggling, unrecognized genius.

Jack's sense of identity is therefore highly unstable, and by the end of the novel, it is virtually extinguished by the eruption of uncontrollable rage and madness. In this situation, he acts without conscious motivation, and is described as a kind of murderous automaton. His actions are not dictated by any sense of self, but seem to be almost automatic or compulsive forms of behaviour. In this way, the novel foregrounds the problem of distinguishing the internal from the external, and this is related to its supernatural elements. If the Overlook Hotel acts upon Jack, it does so by stimulating internal insecurities and anxieties, rather than possessing him in any simple sense.

II   The End of Civilization as We Know It: Apocalyptic Horror

Night of the Living Dead (1968) has also been read as an example of family horror,[28] but it is part of a more general tendency within contemporary horror – apocalyptic horror. It concerns a plague of zombification which threatens to destroy not only the family, but social order in general. Most of the narrative concerns a group of people who spend a night trying to defend themselves against a horde of zombies. Almost all the action takes place within an isolated house which they have boarded-up, but the film clearly places this situation within the context of a national, and probably global, battle against the zombies. Like most other apocalyptic horror narratives of the 1960s and 1970s, the threat is not merely external, but also internal. Indeed it might be said to be self-inflicted. The plague of zombies, it is suggested, are the result of radiation from an American satellite on its return to earth. As the probable source of the problem, the authorities cannot offer any real solution. They argue amongst themselves, and are presented as virtually powerless in the face of the crisis. In fact, the only cure which they offer seems at least as bad as the disease. Posses are sent out to wipe out the zombies, but they are presented as at least as brutal, callous and unthinking as the beings which they are out to destroy. Furthermore, when they finally do arrive at the house where the main characters have been defending themselves against the zombies, they indiscriminately shoot the last survivor of the group.

It is within this context that the family horror aspects of the film work. Just as the social order around them is in crisis, redundant, and riddled with conflicts, so are the relationships between those within the house. Rather than coming together as a coherent group with a shared sense of community, they fight amongst themselves. The situation does not bring out the best in them, but only the worst. In fact, few of them are actually killed as a result of the zombies outside. They are either killed by one another, or as a result of their own incompetence. Even those characters who are killed by a zombie have a familial relationship with the zombie in question. One woman is killed by her own daughter, and another by her brother. For Wood, for example, this highlights the eruption of conflicts and resentments within the family, which is more generally presented as a brutal and oppressive institution.

The film's use of the zombie as a monster is also significant in this regard. Prior to *Night of the Living Dead*, the zombie was a very minor horror monster, but since 1968, it has become one of the major figures in contemporary horror. Its importance is due to its lack of consciousness or conscious motivation, and this is linked to issues of rational control, particularly consumerism. This link is merely hinted at in the original film, but the sequel makes it far more explicit. This follow-up, *Dawn of the Dead* (1978), is set in a shopping mall to which the zombies are drawn by a mindless compulsion which has its roots in the consumer behaviour of their earlier existence as living human beings. This mindlessly compulsive behaviour and lack of conscious motivation is that which links the zombie with other contemporary monsters, but it also links it with the people within the house in *Night of the Living Dead*. These human beings are largely presented as stereotypical or stock characters who lack self-consciousness or imagination. Even in the midst of the siege, they rely on television to give them information about their situation and the appropriate responses to that situation.

Michael Crichton's novel, *The Andromeda Strain* (1969), is another example of apocalyptic horror, and it too concerns a satellite which returns to earth and brings with it a plague that threatens human existence. The main story concerns the attempt by a group of scientists – the Wildfire team – to prevent it from destroying the world. Unlike *Night of the Living Dead* though, the problem is not the internal crisis of the system, but that it is too ordered. The satellite does not bring back a plague by mere accident, but has been sent into space with the explicit aim of discovering plagues for use by the military. If the family is one of the central institutions within contemporary horror, the military is the other. It has come to represent the most destructive aspects of the state for two reasons.

First, it deals with forces of incredible destructive potential such as nuclear and biological weapons, and minor errors can have dramatic effects. In fact, *The Andromeda Strain* goes further. It suggests that rational systems of control have an inherent tendency to crisis. They are inflexible and rigid, and are unable to account for every eventuality. Personal idiosyncrasies, and minor malfunctions create unpredictable havoc within the novel, which also emphasizes that any system will inevitably create its own blindspots. Every system of procedures will inevitably exclude certain options. The novel is a virtual catalogue of blindspots which result in missed opportunities, and one blindspot in particular nearly results in the destruction of the entire world. The research station has been built on the assumption that any plague can be destroyed by intense heat, and it has been fitted with a nuclear device which is programmed to detonate if the plague escapes. No-one has predicted that the plague may actually thrive on energy, and that such an explosion might create the perfect conditions for its almost limitless reproduction.

Second, the military is seen as threatening in contemporary horror by reason of its specific relationship to the population. For reasons of national security, the population has been increasingly denied knowledge of military actions and procedures since World War II. This situation is made clear in the opening of the novel where the military use a rather crude method to detect the satellite for fear of arousing public suspicion about their activities. The novel is filled with such cases. Not only was the actual mission of the satellite kept secret, but the laboratories where the Wildfire team work are disguised as an agricultural research station. Rather than acting in the interests of the population, the novel presents the military as a rational system of control which imposes itself upon them, and which is quite willing to accept the deaths of millions of Americans as part of its rational calculations. The population exist merely to be ordered and controlled.

Like most apocalyptic horror texts, *Night of the Living Dead* and *The Andromeda Strain* do not resolve all the problems at the end of the narrative. At the end of the first, it remains unclear whether the posse will actually succeed in destroying the zombies, but even if it does, all the main characters are dead and the posse hardly represent the promise of a positive or appealing future. In the second, the plague does not destroy humanity, but it continues to have unpredictable effects on human activities. As the final line of the novel states, future developments are 'out of our hands'.[29]

These open endings are partly the result of the loss of confidence in effective action and in authorities which Tudor identified in contemporary horror. If authorities are often the source of the problem, they cannot also be the solution. In contemporary horror, attempts to resolve the situation often fail, or only make matters worse. But there is another aspect which frequently makes narrative resolutions unsatisfying. In a social world which is increasingly seen as a nightmare of regulation and control, it can be pleasurable to witness that world destroy itself.

The Omen (1976), for example, is an apocalyptic horror film which was part of the 1970s preoccupation with demonic forces. It concerns a family who come to realize that their adopted son is, in fact, the Antichrist. Again the issue of apocalypse is linked to the American state: the family in which the Antichrist is raised is that of the American ambassador to London. The film revolves around the father's acquisition of the knowledge necessary to kill his demonic son, Damian. At the end of the film though, he fails in his task. He is shot as he tries to kill his son, and we are left with a final image which suggests that Damian has been adopted by the American President himself.

While this is the nominal plot, and the father is the nominal hero, it is probably more accurate to read the film's plot as being concerned with the inexorable rise to power of the young Damian. The father's death is only the last in a series of grisly deaths which are inflicted on anyone who attempts to organize against Damian. The film also presents these deaths with such relish that Robin Wood has suggested that the film's real pleasure is that of watching Damian systematically destroying contemporary society. As Wood puts it: 'The Omen would make no sense in a society that was not prepared to enjoy and surreptitiously endorse the working out of its own destruction.'[30]

It is this desire to be rid of the existing social world which can also be identified in a sub-genre of apocalyptic horror – the post-apocalypse film. In films such as The Omega Man (1971), A Boy and His Dog (1975), Damnation Alley (1977), and the Mad Max trilogy, there is a clear pleasure in the post-apocalypse world where there may be horrors, but where one is freed from the more mundane forms of control and constraint which distinguish contemporary society. It also allows for the possibility of starting society over again, but getting things right this time. In fact, this is often the explicit narrative problem of post-apocalyptic narratives, and it is one which preoccupies Stephen King's epic post-apocalyptic novel, The Stand (1978).

As in many of these narratives, a plague which has been developed by the military is accidentally released, and proceeds to kill 99.9% of the population. The majority of the novel then concerns the conflict between the survivors as they come together in two distinct groups and struggle to define the nature of a future society. As Stephen King writes in an attempt to explain the pleasure which he experienced in the writing of the novel: 'Much of the compulsion I felt while writing The Stand obviously came from envisioning an entire entrenched societal process destroyed at a stroke. I felt a bit like Alexander, lifting his sword over the Gordian knot and growling, "Fuck untying it. I've got a better way."'[31] Despite this pleasure, he also notes: 'My own lesson in writing The Stand was that cutting the Gordian Knot simply destroys the riddle instead of solving it, and the book's last line is an admission that the riddle still remains.'[32] The riddle is: how can human beings develop ways of living together which are satisfying and fulfilling to all? Destroying existing society may get rid of specific forces which control and oppress people, but it does not, of itself, offer a solution to that riddle.

III Body/Horror

The preoccupation with plagues within apocalyptic horror is also related to another aspect of contemporary horror which is often referred to as 'body/horror'. The texts which are grouped together under this heading are primarily concerned with processes of bodily transformation. The body is either engulfed by some larger process, or else moves towards fragmentation and collapse. These processes can have apocalyptic implications. In certain films, the whole of society is overtaken by their effects. But the focus of concern is mainly upon their impact on an individual and their sense of identity. In this way, these films also concern the instability of identity, though they concentrate mainly upon the sense of bodily identity, rather than consciousness. Their most significant moments are those in which an individual watches their own body change. The sense of identity is also challenged by the loss of any clear sense of an inside or an outside to the body. The threat is not clearly external, but erupts from within the body itself. Despite this, it is usually the result of certain forms of rational control associated with medicine, science, and even the media.

The figure most clearly associated with this aspect of horror is the Canadian film director, David Cronenberg, who has not only worked within Hollywood, but had considerable influence upon the development of American horror. In his first major film, *Shivers* (a.k.a. *They Came From Within*, 1975), he reworks Romero's *Night of the Living Dead* so that the plague is a scientifically generated organism which penetrates the body and turns its victims into pleasure-driven zombies who pass on the organism through sexual contact. Despite its similarities to Romero's film, *Shivers* is far more interested in the processes of biological transformation, and it uses new special effects techniques to depict them.

His next film, *Rabid* (1977), is very similar, but on a much larger scale. It concerns a young women who undergoes a radical new type of surgery as doctors try to save her life. Unfortunately, this surgery gives rise to a strange bodily mutation. The woman develops a phallic spike in one of her armpits, and finds that she can only feed through the use of this spike, which stabs those she embraces, and sucks their blood. As it does so, it also passes on a new strain of rabies which quickly converts its victim into a cannibalistic zombie who passes the plague on to its victims. Soon the plague of rabies is spreading out of control. Despite the larger scope of this film, it is actually more intimate than *Shivers*. The film is mainly interested in the working of the disease, and its effect upon the young woman as she finds herself unable to control her bodily processes.

Cronenberg's films have often come under attack for supposedly displaying a profoundly conservative fear of the body and female sexuality in particular; and they are often interpreted as a conservative reaction to the sexual revolution.[33] Barbara Creed, for example, has argued that the sub-genre as a whole 'reveals a fascination with the maternal body – its inner and outer appearance, its functions, its awesome powers.'[34] Cronenberg's visual style in particular is claimed to be deeply voyeuristic, and to view the body with a horrified, distanced, and controlling gaze. This kind of criticism tends to miss the sense of pleasure with which Cronenberg treats his subjects. He has often stated his sympathy and admiration for the bodily processes with which he deals. Furthermore, while these processes are related to issues of sexuality, they are clearly connected to issues of rational control. The development of bourgeois society came to define the body as an inalienable form of private property which guaranteed individuals a sense of self; but as society was increasingly organized according to rational principles, the body came to be an object of rational control. It is regulated by a whole series of institutions, and as Christopher Lasch has argued in relation to the development of medical institutions, these institutions do not simply act to improve peoples' lives, but 'increase patients' dependence on machines and medical experts who operate these "life-support systems." '[35]

These institutions not only alienate and objectify the body, they make it increasingly difficult to distinguish the body from systems of control. Forms such as spare-part surgery, reproductive technology, and gene-splicing make it increasingly clear that the body is no longer a private sphere, but is increasingly penetrated by a whole series of processes. If these films are concerned with sexuality, it is within this context. Sexual contact also blurs distinctions between the inside and the outside of the body, and between the self and others. Not only is this the case, but as *Shivers* and *Videodrome* (1982) make clear, sexuality is no longer a threat to the system of control, but integrated into it and stimulated by it.

Videodrome is one of Cronenberg's most analysed films. It concerns the head of a pornographic cable channel who spends his time in an attempt to track down a specific piece of sado-masochistic pornography of which he can only discover brief snippets. This televisual image turns out to be part of a plot, and has been used to programme him. It affects his consciousness through his body. In one particularly famous sequence, his body develops a opening into which he is encouraged to insert a video cassette. His body has become an object programmed and controlled by the pornographic media, and the sexual imagery has been used to make his body more receptive to its subliminal stimulations.

The influence of Cronenberg's body/horror films, and the special effects techniques which they pioneered, have been huge. In the late 1970s and 1980s, a series of werewolf films were made which used special effects to show the transformation sequences in extraordinary detail. But despite their relative success, their influence was limited. The dual personality theme of the werewolf narrative did not really develop the body/horror subgenre, and the films tended to rely on references back to classic werewolf films such as *The Wolf Man* (1941) and others.

Alien (1979), on the other hand, used body/horror special effects and concerns in a way that was both highly popular and deeply influential. The film concerns a group of workers on a space cargo vessel who are ordered to investigate what appears to be a distress signal from an alien planet. They find a giant space ship, the insides of which are organic in appearance, and contain a huge chamber filled with alien eggs. One crew member, Kane, is attacked or 'contaminated' by something from within one of the eggs, which wraps itself around his face, and cannot be removed. Eventually, it comes off, but later, Kane starts to cough and convulse. His chest heaves, and an alien being suddenly bursts from inside him before escaping into the ship. From then on, the film presents a fairly straightforward situation in which the crew are killed off one by one. Finally, Ripley, the last survivor, manages to destroy the creature which has now transformed itself into something much bigger and nastier than the thing that emerged from Kane's chest.

There is considerable discussion of this film from a variety of perspectives,[36] but it is the alien species which really distinguishes the film, and was its main influence. It is presented as a kind of biological machine which dominates other species and uses them as a vessel for its own reproduction. In this way, the threat is made both external and internal. The most famous and best remembered sequence is the one in which Kane 'gives birth' to the alien, and it is this aspect which recurs again and again in later science fiction/horror films. As Barbara Creed has claimed, many 1980s science fiction/horror films concern the conversion of the body into a kind of womb from which a new, alien life-form is born.[37]

The film also sets up a series of associations between the corporate/military authorities and the alien. It becomes clear that the authorities have known about the alien species from the start, and that they are exploiting the crew, using them to test the destructive capabilities of the alien which they hope to use as a form of biological weapon. The representatives of these authorities are the ship's computer and the science officer, Ashe, who turns out to be an android. Not only do they share the alien's cold-blooded attitude towards the crew, but also its ambiguous nature. They all complicate distinctions between organic life and machines in various ways, and act to dominate and control the crew.

But if many have praised *Alien* as a radical horror film, it is also related to developments in the 1980s which are often seen as highly conservative, particularly the stalker or slasher film and the re-emergence of the science fiction/horror film. It is these developments which will be the subject of the next chapter.

4. Horror in the 1980s

I The Slasher Movie and the Serial Killer

If the developments of the 1960s and 1970s achieved a measure of critical recognition, and were identified in some quarters as potentially radical, the developments of the late 1970s and 1980s have provoked widespread hostility from critics and reviewers. The 'video nasties' caused a moral panic in both Britain and America, though no clear definition of the term was ever produced. Instead these moral panics largely relied on arguments about the Slasher movie, a subgenre which emerged in America in the late 1970s and early 1980s and provoked considerable hostility. For many critics such as Wood, the slasher movie represented a reactionary turn in contemporary horror.[38] Rather than presenting the monster as a product of American social life, it is claimed that they present the monster as 'the essence of pure evil', an inexplicable destructive force which assaults American social life, but does not imply any criticism of its institutions.[39]

It is the attitude towards women that is believed to be present in these films which is considered their most worrying feature however. Slasher movies concern a serial killer who tracks down a group of teenagers, killing them off one by one in various grisly ways, and it is usually argued that its attacks are primarily directed against women. Even when the number of men killed is equal to the number of women, it is pointed out that it is the killing of women on which these films concentrate.[40] The men are either dispatched quickly, or else their deaths are not seen at all. It is also claimed that the killer's primary target is the women, and that the men are simply killed as a means to this end.

The ways in which the killings are presented are claimed to make this situation even more worrying. One of these films' most distinctive stylistic features is the use of the subjective camera shot from the killer's point of view, and this is reputed to create an identification between the audience and the killer, by placing the audience in the position of the killer rather than its victim.[41] It is also claimed that the women who are killed have usually been engaged in sexual activity just before their deaths, and that their slaughter is presented as a justified punishment for their overt sexuality. Female sexuality is claimed to be threatening to patriarchal culture, so that these films act to contain it by presenting the sexually active women who are killed as merely 'getting what they deserve'. Robin Wood, for example, has argued that these films are a conservative reaction against the women's movement in which 'the women who are terrorized and slaughtered are those who resist definition within the virgin/wife/mother framework.'[42] It is also claimed, in support of this argument, that the women who do survive these films are usually presented as virgins. They are sexually innocent and do not display a threatening female sexuality.

There are a number of problems with these arguments though. First, the objection that the killers are presented as almost inhuman personifications of evil tends to miss the point. Their lack of conscious motivation and their apparently relentless and compulsive types of behaviour not only links them with other monsters in contemporary horror such as the shark in *Jaws* (1975) and the creature in *Alien*, but it is that which makes them both terrifying and fascinating. Critics such as Wood and Newman compare these serial killers with those in films such as *Psycho* and novels such as *The Silence of Lambs* (1988) where the killer's family background is explicitly presented,[43] but even in these cases, the killers are interesting specifically because these explanations are insufficient and do not help people in dealing with them. These figures captivate their audiences because they are driven by relentless and compulsive types of behaviour over which they have no conscious control. The tendencies to refer to these figures as 'killing machines' is therefore highly appropriate. They lack subjectivity and seem to act like programmed automatons. The fears associated with these serial killers are similar to those discussed in relation to other forms of contemporary horror. They are fears that human identity is being erased by forms of rationalized behaviour.

Second, not only do these killers lack consciousness, they also lack all forms of personality. This lack is emphasized by their use of masks. The killer rarely has a human face. For this reason, it is difficult to see how the audience is supposed to identify with them, despite the use of the subjective camera shot. It is difficult to identify with something which is specifically defined by its lack of an identity. This problem is highlighted by Carol J. Clover who points out that the subjective camera shot is used in a variety of different films, such as *Jaws* and *The Birds* (1963), where the point of view is that of animals such as the shark or the birds. As a result, she questions claims about the effect of these techniques and argues 'either that the viewer's identificatory powers are unbelievably elastic or the point-of-view shots can sometimes be pro forma.'[44] In fact, in many slasher movies, the subjective camera shot does not necessarily imply the presence of any being at all, but only its potential presence. There are a whole series of sequences in which it is used to suggest a character's fear that they are being watched, or their vulnerability.

These problems have led some critics to claim that the use of the subjective camera shot is not used to create an identification with the character of the killer, but with the position of the killer.[45] It is used to make us identify with the killer's gaze and the aggression with which it is associated. One problem with this argument is that even if this were the intention, it may not actually work in this way. In 1946, George Montgomery used the subjective camera shot in his film, *The Lady in the Lake*, in an attempt to approximate the first person narrations used by Raymond Chandler in his original novel. The film is very interesting, but it fails in its use of the subjective camera shot. It not only denies the audience any sense of interiority to the character from whose point of view the action is presented, but as a result, it may also have alienated the audience from that character's position. Denied any real access to the character, the gaze itself may become an image from which the audience feel distanced and detached.

A similar problem is also emphasized in John Carpenter's script for *The Eyes of Laura Mars* (1978), a script which he wrote around the same time as his deeply influential slasher movie, *Halloween* (1978). In this film, a woman finds that she has telepathic powers which link her with a serial killer. When he kills, she is denied her own sight, but is forced to watch the killings through the killer's eyes, an experience which is presented as terrible and disabling. She is forced to see that which she does not want to see, and is rendered powerless and helpless both by its imposition upon her and by her inability to prevent the carnage which she witnesses. In this way, she can be seen to occupy a very similar position to that of the audience in a slasher film. The technique may work at times specifically to elicit the feeling of helplessness before the image of the gaze which Laura Mars experiences in Carpenter's narration, rather than an identification with that gaze.

There are also problems with the claims about the attitudes towards women in such films. It may be true that women are the primary targets of the killer, but this need not necessarily imply that the films suggest that the killings are a justified punishment for female sexuality. As Tudor argues in relation to *Halloween*, the most discussed of the slasher movies, 'all three women are appealingly characterized – there is no sense that their activities are inappropriate or immoral. They are frivolous, perhaps, but hardly figures who can be seen as inviting their terrible fates.' [46] In fact, their sexual activity is not presented as threatening to men at all. It is presented as normal teenage behaviour, and something which the males expect of them. By contrast, it is the surviving female, Laurie, who is presented as threatening to men. Her friends are constantly joking that she has 'scared another one away'. The males are intimidated by her intelligence, seriousness, and independence, and it is these qualities that distinguish her in the film, not her virginity. She is clearly interested in men sexually, but is not prepared to accept the role of sexual plaything which the other girls put up with. They are clearly irritated by the males' treatment of them, but accept it as 'normal'. Nor does she disapprove of extra–marital sex, and even denies she is a virgin.

In fact, it is masculinity, not femininity, which is the problem within these films. As Tudor argues, 'however restricted our understanding of the psychotic's motivation ... we are left with the feeling that threatening psychosis is sexual in some way and that male aggression and misogyny are significant elements within it.'[47] The problem of masculinity is also registered in other ways. First, there is a distinct absence of positive or effective male figures within these films. It is the female characters themselves who fight the killer. If male characters do appear, they are usually entirely ineffective. The psychologist in *Halloween*, for example, spends most of the time in the wrong places, and when he finally does track the killer down he is no more effective than Laurie. While Laurie has spent a considerable amount of time in hand to hand combat with the killer, the psychologist is too scared to approach him. Instead he nervously shoots at him, but proves no more effective in killing him.

This absence of these male characters is part of the more general crisis of confidence in authority in American society, a crisis which can also be detected in other aspects. These films frequently present 'normal' everyday life as inherently fragile and unstable. It masks uncontrollably destructive forces which constantly threaten to erupt from within, without apparent explanation. For this reason, these films rarely reach a definitive resolution. Not only is the killer often virtually indestructible, but even when it is killed, the ending is rarely a happy one. It usually depicts the female survivor suffering a virtual breakdown as the result of her experience. She may have survived, but she is only left with a sense of the insecurity and fragility of existence.

It is this loss of faith in authority which displaces traditional male authority figures from the role of the hero, and leads to the emergence of the female hero. This situation does not mean that these films are necessarily feminist texts, but time and again, they are presented as the only figures with the resources to combat and defeat him. In fact as Carol Clover claims while these films may involve some form of identification with the killer at the start, this situation is reversed by the end of the film so that the female hero becomes the main point of identification. More significantly, this reversal also coincides with her appropriation of the gaze. It is often claimed that the 'active, investigating gaze' is defined as male within popular cinema, but this claim is inappropriate to the slasher film where, as Clover argues:

> The gaze becomes, at least for a while, female. More to the point, the female exercise of scopic control results not in her annihilation, in the manner of classic cinema, but in her triumph; indeed her triumph depends on her assumption of the gaze.[48]

In fact, it is her appropriation of the gaze which distinguishes her. As we have seen, the distinguishing feature of female heroes in films such as *Halloween* is not their sexual innocence but their seriousness, intelligence and independence.

In the process, she not only appropriates the traditionally male gaze, but also traditionally male forms of action and heroism. For this reason, as Carol Clover claims, they challenge traditional associations between sex and gender. They do not present women's roles as being determined by their biology, and they enable them to perform activities usually restricted to males. But though these women perform traditionally male activities, this does not mean that these films privilege masculinity as is often claimed. These women are valued, but not because they act like men. Women do not have to become like men to become successful and positive. As Carol Clover points out, it is not masculinity which is privileged, but 'masculinity in conjunction with a female body – indeed, as the term victim-hero contemplates, masculinity in conjunction with femininity.'[49] Male authority remains the problem, and it is the female who refuses her role as victim and rejects the positions of powerlessness associated with femininity who is the hero. Masculine attributes such as aggression, violence, and self-assertion are only positive when they have been reappropriated by those who are usually victims of them.

II The Science Fiction/Horror Film in the 1980s

Many of these developments can also be identified in the science fiction/horror films of the 1980s which became one of the most popular and influential aspects of the genre. In this context, the work of the writer/director James Cameron and his ex-wife, producer Gale Anne Hurd, are exemplary. Their films, particularly *The Terminator* (1984) and *Aliens* (1986), are almost summations of contemporary horror. They contain strong female leads; an interest in the family; concerns about scientific-technical rationality and the military; killing machines which lack conscious motivation; and forms of body/horror. In *The Terminator*, a cyborg killer is sent to present day Los Angeles from the future in order to kill a young woman, Sarah Conner. This cyborg killer, the terminator of the title, is related to the serial killer of the slasher movie both by its actions, and by the film's use of the subjective camera shot from the terminator's point of view. In *The Terminator* though, it is made quite explicit that the fear evoked by the serial killer is a fear of mindless, compulsive, rationalized behaviour. The terminator is half human, and half machine. If most serial killers use masks to hide their human faces, the terminator uses human flesh to hide its mechanized, robotic body.

Not only is the terminator quite literally a killing machine, it is also an extension of scientific-technical rationality and American militarization. The terminator is a product of the American missile systems. In the future, the American defense network computers come to see all human life as a threat and attempt to exterminate humanity. If earlier forms of rationalization had defined the individual qualities of the worker as a source of error that had to be eliminated, the machines of the future come to define humanity itself as a source of error that has to be eliminated; a source of error that can now be replaced by machines. None the less, the film suggests that this redefinition is only a logical extension of current forms of rationalization. The roots of the nightmarish future lie in the mechanized modern cities of contemporary America.

Within the film these modern cities are dominated by machines. They regulate people's work and leisure activities, and the terminator is able to use communications systems such as telephones, telephone books, and answering machines to identify Sarah. The implications of this situation are suggested by the identification number which Kyle, the guerrilla fighter from the future, has imprinted into his flesh, a mark which Constance Penley aptly identifies as 'the ubiquitous bar code stamped on today's consumer items.' [50] Not only are people identified through these machines, they are also identified with them. Sarah's flatmate, Ginger, is never separated from her walkman; and the only feature which seems to distinguish Sarah's unseen boyfriend is the Porsche which he owns.

Within this world, it is difficult to distinguish the human from the machine, the organic from the inorganic. If the terminator is a machine which wears human flesh to disguise itself, human beings are frequently encased within mechanical constructions. It is also a world in which people act in ways that are almost robotic. They are caught up in compulsive, repetitive forms of behaviour. In such a world, the terminator does not seem too out of place. It can calculate and predict the appropriate forms of behaviour and pass for human. In *Terminator 2* (1991), these implications are made even more explicit. The humans are often more insensitive and unthinking than the reprogrammed cyborg sent back to protect John Conner, Sarah's son. This cyborg learns the human emotions and values with which most of the humans within the film have lost contact. As a consequence, Sarah recognizes that 'in an insane world' such as the present, the terminator will make a better, more caring father for her son, John, than any man she has known.

Despite the difficulty of distinguishing the human from the machine, the film does not suggest that distinctions between the two are impossible, or even undesirable, or that humanity and its machines have become replicas of one another. If this were the case, humans would not pose a threat to the machines, and there would be no reason to fear the machines or the possibility of human extinction. The process of rationalization suppresses the individual qualities of the worker in favour of abstract measurements of quantity. It seeks to standardize workers and make them interchangable with one another. By contrast, *The Terminator* associates humanity with those very features suppressed by rationalization, particularly sexual desire and interaction. For example, it is Kyle's desire for Sarah that distinguishes him from the terminator. Rather than defining humanity according to a fixed presence, it is associated with absence; desire is based upon the fact that one's self is incomplete by itself and needs to interact with others.

These issues are addressed through the film's preoccupation with reproduction. The terminator is a product of an asexual process of mechanical reproduction in which human flesh is mass produced as standardized product. It is a product of a monological, rational order, and can never attain an interactive relationship with others of its kind. They are all replicas of one another, and merely follow the programming of the computer systems which produced them. It is only through reprogramming and interaction with humans that the cyborg in *Terminator 2* is able to be 'humanized'. By contrast, Sarah, the terminator's target in the original film, is dangerous to the machines specifically because of her reproductive capabilities. The film stresses that human reproduction, unlike mechanical reproduction, is based on interaction. The child is a product of two human beings and can learn to differentiate itself from its parents through a process of interaction.

In *The Terminator*, the process of rationalized, mechanical reproduction is associated with excessive masculinity through the body of Arnold Schwarzenegger. In *Aliens*, it is associated with a mechanized femininity. The alien mother is a giant reproductive machine. But even in *Aliens*, there is an association with masculinity and the military. The alien species is identified as the 'ideal' soldier, a pure killing machine which is not distracted from its functioning by individual features or desires. This alien species, like the military/corporate state of the humans, is a colonial power. It penetrates other species and transforms them into a vessel for its own reproduction, just as the humans place 'atmosphere processing plants' on alien planets in order to create the conditions necessary for colonization. By converting the human body into a mere vessel for their own reproduction, the aliens are also related to patriarchy which has traditionally defined women as a mere vessel for the reproduction of the male seed. It is for this reason that it is a woman who is not only the aliens' main adversary, but the figure with the resources required to resist them. She rejects rationalization and mechanical reproduction which define human beings, and particularly women, as objects or vessels to be used and controlled. She also highlights the active female component in human reproduction which male forms of authority deny or repress. She stands for interaction in opposition to rationalized order. Within these films, it is women, not men, who represent that which is truly human.

This presentation of women does not operate to confirm women in the tradition role of mothers. While Constance Penley claims that these films confine women to the role of mother,[51] Barbara Creed claims that in *Aliens*, Ripley is not really a woman at all.[52] She argues that Ripley undergoes the male passage through the Oedipus complex in the film. By destroying the alien mothers' genitals with a phallic gun, Ripley is construed as separating herself from the maternal, and identifying with masculine positions within culture. Both Penley and Creed's claims sound credible, but both ignore aspects of female heroes such as Sarah and Ripley. While these female characters are associated with the maternal, they also perform activities which are usually associated with masculinity. When Ripley aims that phallic gun at the mother's genitals, she is also engaged in the maternal protection of a surrogate daughter. These female heroes are distinguished by their hybridity. They erase distinctions between masculine and feminine activities in similar ways to the female heroes in the Slasher film, and transform the meaning of maternity and violent action through the course of the films.

In *The Terminator*, Sarah is not an image of self-sacrificing motherhood, but the source of her son's strength and authority. Everything he is comes from her, and she is the myth that holds the resistance of the future together. Despite the film's mythic elements – John Conner has the same initials as Jesus Christ, and his conception is an impossible, almost immaculate one – Sarah is not presented as a virgin mother like the Madonna. It is Kyle, John's father, who is the virgin. If Sarah does become a myth for the future, the film does not present the audience with the myth of Sarah, but Sarah herself. The film allows the audience to watch a process of mythologization which is not imposed upon Sarah by men, but is engineered by Sarah as she narrates her story to John.

Most of these features remain central to *Terminator 2*, though it both extends and limits features of the original film. While Sarah starts off as a victim in the original film, but slowly comes to recognize her own potential, she is both stronger and more peripheral in the sequel. Defined as insane by society, she is presented as the only sane person in an insane world as she struggles to halt humanity's drive towards self-destruction. The newly acquired star status of Schwarzenegger tends to undermine her centrality however, as does the mission of the new terminator. This time, it is the young John, not Sarah who is the terminator's target. For example, while it is clear that Sarah is capable of defeating the new terminator at the end of the film, it is Schwarzenegger who ultimately saves the day. For once, the contemporary female hero does not save herself in the last instance, but is saved by a 'male' hero.

None the less, male authority figures are still problems within the film, as is shown by way in which the new terminator continually disguises itself as a Los Angeles Police officer, to say nothing of the way in which psychiatrists, SWAT teams, scientists, and company managements are presented. Not only does the film carefully distance Schwarzenegger from positions of authority and place his character in the 'feminized' position of John's self-sacrificing and nurturing protector (in contrast to Sarah's masculinized authoritative female), it also needs to destroy him at the end. Not only is he a potential threat to the future of humanity – he is destroyed so that no trace of the future will remain –

but also to Sarah and John's independence. The film cannot completely separate him from associations with male authority, but it resists the suggestion that John and Sarah will come to rely on him.

A similar problem emerges in relation to Sarah. She has acquired combat skills and become a tough, female warrior, but the film has to resist the suggestion that women have to become like men to achieve success. She must be separated from associations with male authority and domination, and this is achieved in two main ways. First, she is continually haunted by dreams of the nuclear annihilation which she knows is coming. Her actions are placed in opposition to the destructive forms of violence and domination which will cause human self-destruction. Her use of violent action is a resistance against the dominance of scientific-technical rationality and American militarization. Second, she learns to distinguish herself from forms of male authority through the course of the narrative. She discovers the name of the scientist who will develop the technology responsible for the machines of the future, and she decides to change the future by killing him. In the attempt, she becomes the mirror image of the terminator in the first film, and as a result, she finds that she is finally unable to kill the scientist. Instead she collapses into an almost cataleptic state. It is only as she is coaxed out of this state by John that she is finally able to interact with her son. Obsessed by the future, she has lost contact with her feelings for her son, and her ability to interact with him. She has become authoritarian as she tries to train him for his future role, and she has defined their personal feelings as secondary to his future mission. This behaviour has caused John pain earlier in the film, particularly after he has tried to save her from the mental institution in which the authorities have imprisoned her. By rejecting the role of the terminator, she dissociates herself from masculine positions, and rediscovers the importance of human feeling and interaction.

If Sarah, John, and the terminator do form a kind of family group during the film, it is one which is clearly distinguished from the 'normal', patriarchal family of middle class America. There is no clear authority figure – certainly no patriarch – and they are placed in clear distinction to the 'normal', middle class, suburban family who act as John's foster parents at the beginning of the film. If Sarah, John, and the terminator compose an ideal family group, it is one which is made up of a mother whom society has defined as insane, a son who is a juvenile delinquent, and a father who is a robot.

III   Contemporary Horror Fiction by Women

These developments may not be inherently radical, but they are related to the development of feminist horror fiction. Gale Anne Hurd often talks of her work in terms of feminism, and has worked to encourage women within Hollywood. In literature too, women writers such as Lisa Tuttle have begun to write self-consciously feminist horror fiction. Horror has always been an important area of women's writing from Ann Radcliffe and Mary Shelley, though the Brontës and Charlotte Gilman Perkins, to contemporary writers such as Angela Carter and Joyce Carole Oates (whose work not only may be read as horror, but who also publishes horror under the pseudonym of Rosamond Smith.) Recently, however, there has been a proliferation of popular women horror writers, some of whom write as feminists and some of whom do not. Unfortunately this is one of the least appreciated aspects of both contemporary horror, and women's writing. Little work has been done on this area, despite the fact that it is a vital area of popular women's writing. Ironically, certain aspects of feminism have been partly responsible for this lack of recognition. Feminist approaches to horror have tended to dismiss the genre too quickly as an inherently patriarchal genre which is primarily produced and consumed by men. As a result, they have tended to ignore its interest and appeal to women writers and female audiences.

For many reasons, women's horror fiction has been much more productive in America than in Britain. Most of it is not even available in this country except on import from the States. One problem is produced by the shape of the British market. Women's horror does not conform to the rather limited definition of horror in Britain, and is often excluded from the image of women's writing perpetuated by feminist publishing houses and critics. Women's Press have begun to publish some women's horror writers. Lisa Tuttle has produced a collection of horror written by women, *Skin of the Soul* (1990), and they have also released Melanie Tem's *Blood Moon* (1992) and Suzy McKee Charnas's *The Vampire Tapestry* (1980). But even these books are hard to find. They are often unavailable in either the horror or women's fiction sections of bookshops. In fact, assumptions about the horror genre often lead publishers and bookshops to reclassify women's horror as either Gothic romance, dark fantasy, or thriller fiction. As Lisa Tuttle has argued: 'It has almost become a circular self-fulfilling argument: horror is written by men, so if it's written by women, it isn't horror.'[53] But if, as a result, men seem to dominate the field of horror novels, the situation in the magazines is quite different. As the horror writer Kathryn Ptacek has claimed in relation to horror fiction, 'when it comes to the short story, women write and publish as regularly as men.'[54]

The forms of women's horror are as various as those of male horror writing, but there are certain specific tendencies which can be discerned within them. One of these is a particular fascination with the figure of the vampire, a horror monster that has largely vanished from male writing. But even within this area, there is immense variety. The most popular of these writers is Anne Rice, whose vampire novels, 'the Vampire Chronicles' – *Interview with the Vampire* (1976), *The Vampire Lestat* (1985), and

Queen of the Damned (1988) – are some of the few examples of women's horror to have gained mainstream popular success outside of cult readerships. Their main characters are usually male vampires, but they are presented as sympathetic and attractive figures whose narratives run parallel to the course of human history. These novels have become particularly popular within the gay community,[55] though their relation to women's fiction is more ambiguous. They do share many features with the historical romance, such as a profound fascination with the details of their romanticized and exotic historical situations, and with different forms of desire. These forms of desire are not primarily sexual, though they may have a sexual aspect, but are often a desire to overcome a feeling of isolation and vulnerability through a close emotional bond with another, and in this way, they have much in common with the dynamics of the romance.

Suzy McKee Charnas's novel, *The Vampire Tapestry*,[56] is also about a male vampire, though he is very different from Rice's vampires. First, he is a lone vampire and is not related to a larger vampire community. Second, the novel is set in the present and gives few details of his existence in previous periods of history. Finally, the novel's attitude to him is much more ambiguous. He is not a particularly romantic figure. He views humans as cattle, and preys upon them in unpleasant ways. In Rice's novels, there is a romantic and appealingly sexual aspect to the vampires' acts, but in Charnas's novel, the vampire's attacks are brutal violations, and are likened to sexual assaults such as rape. The vampire does become a progressively sympathetic figure, but only as he himself is victimized by a group of Satanists who encage and abuse him. During this period, he begins to develop his first positive relationships with humans. He is befriended by young boy who helps him, and this friendship is the start of a process which begins to transform him. As he begins to interact with humans, his perception of himself and his actions gradually changes. The two significant characters in this process are a female psychiatrist with whom he has his first sexual encounter with a human, and a male Satanist who wants to sacrifice the vampire in the belief that this act will give him immense power. These two figures become the positive and negative figures within the book. It is by comparing himself to them that the vampire examines himself. One teaches him the value of interaction, while the other represents the evils of power and victimization.

Nancy Collins's vampire novels differ in various ways, though they are linked by narrative details and figures, particularly the figure of 'Sir Morgan'. Her first and third novels, *Sunglasses After Dark* (1989) and *In the Blood* (1992), are centred on a female vampire, Sonja Blue, who is a complex and relatively sympathetic figure. Her second novel, *Tempter* (1990), on the other hand, concerns a male vampire – the tempter of the title – who is thoroughly depraved and demonic. In this second novel in particular, the use of the vampire raises issues of gender and race. The vampire was once human, and is the product of a depraved and exploitative family background. Cursed by the slaves whose labour built the family's empire, the empire and the family collapse, and the vampire – their last representative – is destroyed by two females who represent those he has exploited. One is the reincarnation of the wife whom he abused, and the other of his daughter. As a slave owner, he had raped and abused a slave who was his wife's maid and companion before selling her to a whorehouse to break the bond between her and his wife. His daughter was a product of that rape.

The larger part of the novel does not take place in the Slave South, however, but in contemporary New Orleans where the vampire tries to reassert his dominance. The women who are the reincarnations of his wife and daughter know nothing of their history – one is a young yuppie, and the other is a member of the city's poor black population – and the story is at least as much about the way in which they discover their power as it is about the vampire. In fact, it is the dilemmas of the young yuppie, Charlie, which are the major focus of the novel, and her character makes it particularly clear that in this novel the threat is not merely external but internal too. Not only is the main feature of the vampire that he is a tempter or trickster who compels people to perform his will by playing upon their own anxieties and desires, but Charlie is a woman who is constantly attracted to men who abuse her. This problem is related to her previous incarnation, Eugenie, whose romantic attachment to her abusive husband resulted in her own death. Both incarnations have internalized male power to such an extent that they have actually learned to desire their own degradation. Charlie's situation also highlights the fact that the problems of male power are not restricted to males of the Slave South, but also a feature of contemporary America. As a result, Charlie's story is not just a confrontation with the vampire, but with her own self-destructive sexuality. In the end, she not only destroys the vampire, but also breaks out of the cycle of abusive relationships which have dominated her past. The victory is not total though. The threat of 'temptation' continues, and must be constantly confronted.

These issues link *Tempter* with a large body of women's horror writing which concerns the problems faced by women within the family in general, and within their relationships with men in particular. Traditionally women have been taught to subjugate their own identities to their husbands and families, and this situation leads many women to experience the family as a place of confinement. Changes in the job market, and the development of feminism since the 1960s, have changed this situation to some extent. Women are now encouraged to realize their own potential, and develop social roles outside the domestic sphere of the family home. These developments do not mean that traditional social roles have vanished though, and frequently women find that a conflict develops between the demands of their traditional social roles, and their newly acquired expectations. Their new-found independence can often conflict with the demands and expectations of families and lovers. Consequently, while the family can still be seen as a realm of restriction and confinement, independence can also be feared as a form of insecurity and isolation.

It is this kind of dilemma which concerns Lisa Tuttle in her novel, *Familiar Spirit* (1983). It concerns a young woman, Sarah, who feels trapped in her relationship with her lover, Brian. In this case though, it is not Brian himself who is the problem. Brian is anything but a domineering male. Instead, the problem is inside Sarah's own personality itself. She finds she cannot help subjugating herself to Brian, and she fears her feelings of emotional and sexual dependency upon him. When she leaves Brian things do not improve though. She feels vulnerable and isolated, and these feelings are made worse when Brian starts seeing someone else almost immediately after Sarah has left him. Suddenly, she feels abandoned and betrayed. Like Charlie in Collins's *Tempter*, Sarah has internalized the paradigms of male power. She cannot help subordinating herself to a man within a relationship, and she feels worthless when she is outside a relationship. These issues of internalized male authority are also dealt with through the novel's horror elements. When Sarah leaves Brian, she rents a house which is possessed by a male spirit, Jade. Much of the book is about Jade's fight to subjugate her, and to take possession of her. Not only does this situation highlight the instability of identity through a concentration on consciousness, but also through her relationship to her own body. As Jade possesses her, she becomes a mere spectator in relation to it. She watches her body act without any control over its actions. It becomes alien to her.

This concern with the alienation of women from their own bodies is common to a number of Lisa Tuttle's stories, and those of other women horror writers. In 'Bug House' (published in Lisa Tuttle, *Nest of Nightmares*, 1986), for example, the implications are made overt through an association with issues of rape and childbearing. Women's bodies are frequently defined as either the property of others, or as objects which exist for the gratification of males or children. This attitude towards women's bodies is common in many aspects of contemporary culture, but it is deeply enshrined in the ideology of the family. In the family, the wife is usually defined as the figure who exists to look after the husband and children, and biologically to reproduce the male line. In 'Bug House', a young women is raped by a man who impregnates her with his seed. This act has two effects. First, it converts her into a host for the insects which will issue from his seed, feed upon her body as they grow, and eventually kill her as they hatch. Second, it renders her body incapable of independent movement. She cannot even feel it. Her body ceases to be her own in any meaningful sense, but becomes something strange and alien which confines her, and which she can only experience as a spectator.

These issues are dealt with in other ways by other women writers. In Kit Reed's 'Baby' (published in Kathryn Ptacek, ed., *Women of Darkness*, 1988), a child is presented as a vampire-like creature which needs to be constantly fed, and these needs not only come to dominate the female character in the story, but also threatens to destroy her. In Melanie Tem's 'Lightening Rod' (published in *Skin of the Soul*, 1990), a woman's body is literally scarred by the tensions in her family. She is a wife and mother who tries to protect her family from pain by absorbing the pain into herself. This role becomes so central to her sense of identity that she cannot bear the idea of her daughter taking over this role from her.

In fact, within these narratives, it is women's investment in their positions of subjugation and subordination which is their most disturbing feature. Frequently, the leading female finally resigns herself to the forces that threaten to oppress her, and surrenders to those forces. The ultimate horror, within this fiction, is that male power may be so pervasive that these female characters not only desire their subordination, but have lost their power to resist it as a consequence.

Conclusion

Horror is usually discussed as a conservative, dangerous and rather abhorrent genre of popular fiction. In response, this brief study has examined its various radical aspects and potentials. The claim most often directed against horror is that it is somehow 'sick'; that its preoccupation with violence and sexuality are excessive and politically reprehensible. As has been pointed out, one of the ironies of this situation are the startling similarities between left-wing and right-wing critics of the genre. It is continually claimed that horror causes anti-social or aggressive behaviour usually directed against women. The genre is supposed to revolve around 'violence against women' and is said to both satisfy and encourage 'unhealthy', sadistic attitudes within the audience. If women are seen as the primary victims in horror, it is also claimed that the monstrous is also directly associated with female sexuality and reproductive capabilities. The genre is supposed to encourage negative images of women in two ways: by presenting their degradation as both exciting and pleasurable; and by presenting women as 'abnormal', frightening and monstrous. Women are supposedly presented as both the victims (who are not only responsible for their fate, but also enjoy it), and as the monster; that which must be contained or repressed.

This study has challenged such responses in two main ways. First, it has contested the claim that any genre has such a fixed and unitary political position. It is certainly true that certain books and films may exhibit the feature criticized above, but genres develop historically according to a process of debate and struggle. They are used and appropriated by different groups with different political interests. As a result, their concerns will not only change and develop, but different films from any particular period will take different position with regard to any specific issues or problems. Second, it is perhaps even more important to stress that those attacking the genre usually rely on highly simplistic and even inaccurate theories about the 'effects' of texts upon their audiences. Such positions present these 'effects' in direct and almost mechanical terms, and pay almost no attention to the conditions within which the consumption of texts take place. As many studies have shown, the process of consumption is far more complex than the 'effects' tradition has acknowledged.

Rather than presenting the genre as a unitary object with a fixed structure or system of structuration, the present study has therefore concentrated on the different ways in which it has developed in America since 1951. It has discussed the ways in which it has dealt with the process of rationalization, or the development of rational control; its critique of American institutions, particularly the family and the military; and its questioning of concepts of 'normality'. In the process, it has also shown how changing modes of social organization have created a crisis of identity in relation to both our sense of ourselves as conscious beings, and the integrity of our bodies. While these issues are frequently related to issues of gender and sexuality, the study has examined the ways in which horror texts have often questioned forms of male power, and so given greater and greater centrality to female characters, particularly in the role of the hero. It is for this reason that horror has not only been such an important and enduring area of women's writing in general, but for radical women writers in particular.

It would be wrong to simply reverse the position of critics of the genre by claiming that horror is not a conservative genre, but a radical one. None the less, its concern with issues of power and victimization has meant that it has always had a strong tendency towards radicalism. But radicalism itself, like the genre, is not a fixed position: what is radical in one period many appear conservative in the next. It is constantly developing and changing, as will the horror genre, at least in the foreseeable future.

Notes

1. Martin Barker, *A Haunt of Fears: The Strange Case of the British Horror Comics Campaign*, Pluto, 1984.
2. Martin Barker, ed., *The Video Nasties: Freedom and Censorship in the Media*, Pluto, 1984.
3. For studies of pornography which are exceptions to this general tendency,

see Linda Williams, *Hard-Core: Power, Pleasure, and the Frenzy of the Visible*, Pandora, 1990; and Andrew Ross, 'The Popularity of Pornography', in *No Respect: Intellectuals and Popular Culture*, Routledge, 1989.

4. See, for example, Ivan Butler, *Horror in the Cinema*, Warner, 1970; and R. H. W. Dillard, *Horror Films*, Monarch, 1976.

5. See, for example, on mass culture theory, Dwight MacDonald, 'Masscult and Midcult', in *Against the American Grain*, Victor Gollancz, 1963; and on post-structuralism, Terry Eagleton, *Literary Theory: An Introduction*, Blackwells, 1983; Terence Hawkes, *Structuralism and Semiotics*, Methuen, 1977; Pam Cook, *The Cinema Book*, BFI, 1985; Robert Lapsley and Michael Westlake, *Film Theory: An Introduction*, Manchester University Press, 1988; and Stephen Neale, *Genre*, BFI, 1980.

6. Stephen Neale, *Genre*, BFI, 1980, p.61.

7. Barbara Creed, 'Horror and the Monstrous-Feminine: An Imaginary Abjection', in James Donald, ed., *Fantasy and the Cinema*, BFI, 1989.

8. Clare Hanson, 'Stephen King: Powers of Horror', in Brian Docherty, ed., *American Horror Fiction: From Brockden Brown to Stephen King*, Macmillan, 1990, p.152.

9. See, for example, Raymond Williams, *Marxism and Literature*, Oxford, 1977; Raymond Williams, *Problems in Materialism and Culture*, Verso, 1980; Raymond Williams, *Culture*, Fontana, 1981; Stuart Hall, 'Deconstructing the Popular', in Raphael Samuel, ed., *People's History and Socialist Theory*, Routledge, 1981; David Morley, 'Changing Paradigms in Audience Studies', in Ellen Seiter *et al.*, eds., *Remote Control: Television, Audiences and Cultural Power*, Routledge, 1989; David Morley, *The Nationwide Audience: Structure and Decoding*, BFI, 1980; David Morley, *Family Television: Cultural Power and Domestic Leisure*, Comedia, 1986; Mark Jancovich, 'David Morley and Audience Studies', in Martin Barker and Anne Beezer, eds., *Reading into Cultural Studies*, Routledge, 1992; and for an account of Cultural Studies in America, see Patrick Brantlinger, *Crusoe's Footprints: Cultural Studies in Britain and America*, Routledge, 1990.

10. Antonio Gramsci, *Selections from the Prison Notebooks*, Lawrence and Wishart, 1971.

11. V. N. Volosinov, *Marxism and the Philosophy of Language*, Seminar, 1973.

12. *Ibid.*, p.23.

13. Pierre Bourdieu, *Distinction: A Social Critique of the Judgement of Taste*, trs. Richard Nice, Routledge and Kegan Paul, 1984; and Raymond Williams and Nicholas Garnham, 'Pierre Bourdieu and the Sociology of Culture: An Introduction', in Richard Collins *et al.*, eds., *Media, Culture and Society*, Sage, 1986.

14. See, for example, Mark Jancovich, *Horror*, Batsford, 1992.

15. See, for example, Robin Wood, *Hollywood from Vietnam to Reagan*, Columbia, 1986; and Peter Biskind, *Seeing is Believing: How Hollywood Taught Us to Stop Worrying and Love the Fifties*, Pluto, 1983.

16. See, for example, David Harvey, *The Condition of Postmodernity: An Enquiry into the Origins of Cultural Change*, Blackwells, 1989.

17. See for example, Daniel Bell, *The End of Ideology*, Collier-Macmillan,

1965; *The Coming of Post-Industrial Society: A Venture in Social Forecasting*, Heinemann, 1974.

18. See C. Wright Mills, *The Power Elite: On the Ruling Groups in the United States*, Oxford, 1956; Dwight MacDonald, 'Masscult and Midcult', in *Against the American Grain, op. cit.*, Herbert Marcuse, *One Dimensional Man: Studies in the Ideology of Advanced Industrial Society*, Beacon, 1964.

19. Georg Lukacs, 'Reification and the Consciousness of the Proletariat', in *History and Class Consciousness: Studies in Marxist Dialectics*, Merlin, 1971, p.89.

20. Jack Finney, *Invasion of the Bodysnatchers*, Sphere, 1978, p.39.

21. See Peter Biskind, *Seeing is Believing*.

22. See Peter Biskind, *Seeing is Believing*.

23. Robin Wood, *Hollywood from Vietnam to Reagan*.

24. Barbara Creed, 'Horror and the Monstrous-Feminine'.

25. Judie Newman, 'Shirley Jackson and the Reproduction of Mothering: The Haunting of Hill House', in Brian Docherty, *American Horror Fiction*.

26. Dwight MacDonald, 'Masscult and Midcult'.

27. Andrew Tudor, *Monsters and Mad Scientists: A Cultural History of the Horror Movie*, Blackwells, 1989.

28. Robin Wood, *Hollywood from Vietnam to Reagan*.

29. Michael Crichton, *The Andromeda Strain*, Dell, 1969, p.291.

30. Robin Wood, *Hollywood from Vietnam to Reagan*.

31. Stephen King, *Danse Macabre*, Futura, 1982, p.449.

32. *Ibid.*, p.451.

33. Robin Wood, 'David Cronenberg: A Dissenting View', in Piers Handling, ed., *The Shape of Rage: The Films of David Cronenberg*, General, 1983.

34. Barbara Creed, 'From Here to Modernity', in *Screen*, Vol.28, No.2, 1987, pp.57.

35. Christopher Lasch, *The Minimal Self: Psychic Survival in Troubled Times*, W. W. Norton, 1979, p.42. See also Peter Boss, 'Vile Bodies and Bad Medicine', *Screen*, Vol.27, No.1, 1986.

36. See, for example, Annette Kuhn, *Alien Zone*, Verso, 1990; and James Donald, ed., *Fantasy and the Cinema*.

37. Barbara Creed, 'From Here to Modernity'.

38. Robin Wood, *Hollywood from Vietnam to Reagan*.

39. Robin Wood, *Ibid.*; Kim Newman, 'Time After Time' in *Fear* No.12 1989.

40. Vera Dika, 'The Stalker Film, 1978–81', in Gregory A. Waller, ed., *American Horrors: Essays on the Modern American Horror Film*, University of Illinois Press, 1987.

41. See, Robin Wood, *Hollywood From Vietnam to Reagan*; and Stephen Neale, 'Halloween: Suspense, Aggression and the Look', in Barry K. Grant, ed., *Planks of Reason: Essays on the Horror Film*, Scarecrow, 1984.

42. Robin Wood, *Hollywood from Vietnam to Reagan*, p.197.

43. Robin Wood, *Hollywood from Vietnam to Reagan*; and Kim Newman, 'Time After Time'.

44. Carol J. Clover, 'Her Body, Himself: Gender in the Slasher Film', in James Donald, ed., *Fantasy and the Cinema*, p.113.

45. Vera Dika, 'The Stalker Film, 1978–81'.

46. Andrew Tudor, *Monsters and Mad Scientists*, p.202.
47. *Ibid.*, p.203.
48. Carol J. Clover, 'Her Body, Himself: Gender in the Slasher Film', pp.124–25.
49. *Ibid.*, p.126.
50. Constance Penley, 'Time Travel, Primal Scene, and the Critical Dystopia', in James Donald, ed., *Fantasy and the Cinema*, BFI, 1989, p.199.
51. *Ibid.*
52. Barbara Creed, 'From Here to Modernity'.
53. Lisa Tuttle, 'Introduction', in *Skin of the Soul*, Women's Press, 1990, p.3.
54. Kathryn Ptacek, 'Introduction', in *Women of Darkness*, Tor, 1988, p.ix.
55. For a discussion of Anne Rice, see Richard Dyer, 'Children of the Night: Vampirism as Homosexuality, Homosexuality as Vampirism', in Susannah Radstone, ed., *Sweet Dreams: Sexuality, Gender, and Popular Fiction*, Lawrance and Wishart, 1988.
56. Anne Cranny-Francis, 'De-Fanging the Vampire: S. M. Charnas's *The Vampire Tapestry* as Subversive Horror Fiction', in Brian Docherty, *American Horror Fiction*.

Bibliography

There are a variety of general books on horror many of which contain material on American horror in the post-war period. One useful resource is *The Penguin Encyclopedia of Horror and the Supernatural* (Viking Penguin, 1986), which is edited by Jack Sullivan. It contains sections on a variety, of books, films, authors and directors, as well as essays on various aspects of the genre. Also useful is David Punter's *The Literature of Terror: A History of Gothic Fictions from 1765 to the Present Day* (Longmans, 1980), which mainly concentrates on canonical literature and dissociates itself from the term 'horror' through the use of the more literary and legitimate term 'gothic' . It has a good chapter on the horror film, and contains other useful material. James Twitchell's *Dreadful Pleasures: An Anatomy of Modern Horror* (Oxford University Press, 1985) is more focussed on popular forms of horror, but tends to be rather reductive, interpreting them in terms of the three classic monsters of the 19th century: the vampire, the werewolf, and Frankenstein's monster. More recently, there have been two general studies of the genre – Noel Carroll's *The Philosophy of Horror: Or Paradoxes of the Heart* (Routledge, 1990) and Joseph Grixti's *The Terrors of Uncertainty: The Cultural Contexts of Horror Fiction* (Routledge, 1989), both highly disappointing. Carroll's book is repetitive, and adds little to the study of the genre. Grixti is not very concerned with the study of actual texts, and is somewhat unconvincing when he is. Grixti's major contribution is that he provides an introduction to the various different studies of the 'effects' of horror fiction. One of the best, and certainly one of the most enjoyable introductions to the genre is Stephen King's *Danse Macabre* (Futura, 1982). While it is not always entirely convincing, it is certainly the most readable introduction available. My own introduction, *Horror* (Batsford, 1992) is also available.

There are a number of different books on the horror film many of which are useful. R. H. W. Dillard's *Horror Films* (Monarch 1976), Ivan Butler's *Horror in the Cinema* (Warner, 1970) and Carlos Clarens's *An Illustrated History of the Horror Film* (Putnam, 1967) are all important, though they mainly concentrate on the period prior to 1970s. Charles Derry's *Dark Dreams: A Psychological History of the Modern Horror Film* (Barnes, 1977) makes more space for the period after 1960, but for a truly comprehensive study of contemporary films one should consult Kim Newman's excellent book, *Nightmare Movies: A Critical History of the Horror Movie From 1968* (Bloomsbury, 1988).

These earlier books are good introductions to general trends, but they are not primarily concerned with a theoretical analysis of the genre. Andrew Tudor does a very good job of combining these two approaches in his book, *Monsters and Mad Scientists: A Cultural History of the Horror Movie* (Blackwells, 1989), and more straightforwardly theoretical approaches can be found in Pam Cook's *The Cinema Book* (BFI, 1985); Stephen Neale, *Genre* (BFI, 1980); and Barbara Creed, *The Monstrous-Feminine: Film, Feminism, Psychoanalysis* (Routledge, 1993). A particularly useful and challenging study is Carol J. Clover, *Men, Women and Chainsaws: Gender in the Modern Horror Film* (London: BFI, 1992). This is an excellent and important book.

Theoretical discussions of specific films, themes and subgenres can also be found in a variety of collections, such as James Donald, *Fantasy and the Cinema* (BFI, 1989), Gregory A. Waller, *American Horror: Essays on the Modern American Horror Film* (University of Illinois Press, 1987), Barry K. Grant, ed., *Planks of Reason: Essays on the Horror Film* (Scarecrow, 1984), and Robin Wood and Richard Lippe, eds., *American Nightmare: Essays on the Horror Film* (Festival of Festivals, 1979). Robin Wood's, *Hollywood from Vietnam to Reagan* (Columbia University Press, 1986) also includes important essays.

There are also several useful studies of specific areas. For example, Peter Biskind's *Seeing is Believing: How Hollywood Taught Us to Stop Worrying and Love the Fifties* (Pluto, 1983) has several good studies of 1950s horror films, and there is a considerable amount of work on body/horror. Piers Handling's *The Shape of Rage: The Films of David Cronenberg* (General, 1983) is a good collection, and Tania Modleski's 'The Terrors of Pleasure: The Contemporary Horror Film and Postmodern Theory' (in Tania Modleski, ed., *Studies in Entertainment: Critical Approaches to Culture*, Indiana University Press, 1986) also discusses the work of David Cronenberg. Barbara Creed's 'From Here to Modernity:

Feminism and Postmodernism' (in *Screen*, Vol.28, No.2, 1987) discusses a variety of body/horror texts, including James Cameron and Gale Anne Hurd's *Aliens*. Peter Boss's 'Vile Bodies and Bad Medicine' (*Screen* Vol.27, No.1, 1986, pp.14–22) also contains a useful discussion of body/horror.

A wealth of material exists on the slasher film including Kim Newman's 'Time After Time' (in *Fear*, No.12, 1989), Stephen Neale's 'Halloween: Suspense, Aggression and the Look' (in Barry K. Grant, ed., *Planks of Reason: Essays on the Horror Film*, Scarecrow, 1984), Vera Dika's, 'The Stalker Film, 1978–1981' (in Gregory A. Waller, ed., *American Horror: Essays on the Modern American Horror Film*, University of Illinois Press, 1987), and most significant of all, Carol J. Clover's 'Her Body, Himself: Gender in the Slasher Film' (in James Donald, ed., *Fantasy and the Cinema*, BFI, 1986). Finally, Constance Penley discusses *The Terminator* in her essay, 'Time Travel, Primal Scene, and the Critical Dystopia' (in James Donald, ed., *Fantasy and the Cinema*, BFI, 1989). It is also worth consulting *The Monthly Film Bulletin* and *Sight and Sound* for discussions of individual films. It is also worth looking out for an edition of *The Velvet Light Trap*, which is dedicated to the horror film and includes my long essay on *The Terminator*, 'Modernity and Subjectivity in *The Terminator*: The Machine as Monster in Contemporary American Culture'.

There is far less work on popular horror literature. Everett Franklin Bleiler's *Supernatural Fiction Writers*, Vols. I & II (Scribners, 1982) contains useful discussions of some of the main writers in the field, as does Darrell Schweitzer's *Discovering Modern Horror Fiction*, Vols. I & II (Starmont 1985). Brian Docherty, *American Horror Fiction: From Brockden Brown to Stephen King*, (Macmillan, 1990) contains some very good individual essays. Douglas E. Winter's *Faces of Fear: Encounter with the Creators of Modern Horror* (Pan, 1990) is a fairly useful, though uncritical, collection of interviews, but there are almost no women writers mentioned within it. As a remedy to this absence, it is worth consulting Kathryn Ptacek's 'Introduction' to her collection *Women of Darkness* (Tor, 1988), and Lisa Tuttle's 'Introduction' to her own collection, *Skin of the Soul*, (Women's Press, 1990).